WINNING THE BATTLE AGAINST MYSELF

WINNING THE BATTLE AGAINST MYSELF

*A Black Woman's Journey Through
America's Corridors of Power*

Trudi Michelle Morrison, PhD, JD

Storytellers Publishing
Colorado, USA

Storytellers Publishing
An imprint of Journey Institute Press,
a division of 50 in 52 Journey, Inc.
journeyinstitutepress.org

Copyright © 2025 Trudi M. Morrison
All rights reserved.
Journey Institute Press supports copyright. Copyright allows artistic creativity, encourages diverse voices, and promotes free speech. Thank you for purchasing an authorized edition of this work and for complying with copyright laws by not reproducing, scanning, or distributing any part of this work in any form without permission.

Library of Congress Control Number: 2024951736
Names: Morrison, Trudi M
Title: WINNING THE BATTLE AGAINST MYSELF
Description: Colorado: Storytellers Publishing, 2025

Identifiers: ISBN 978-1-964754-16-1 (hardcover)
978-1-964754-17-8 (paperback)
978-1-964754-18-5 (ebook/kindle)
Subjects: BISAC:
BIOGRAPHY & AUTOBIOGRAPHY / African American & Black
BIOGRAPHY & AUTOBIOGRAPHY / Women
BIOGRAPHY & AUTOBIOGRAPHY / Memoirs

First Edition

Printed in the United States of America
1 2 3 8 17 23 30 47 69 76

This book was typeset in EB Garamond / Playfair Display

Cover Design by WiggleB Studios

For All My Children

Simone Danielle Ross
Logan Morrison Saunders
Gavin Morrison Ross
Zoe Monroe Ross (My Angel)

Contents

Foreword	ix
Introduction	11
Who Are You? Who Am I?	13
School Daze	26
Oozing Cakes	34
Brown Sugar and Cinnamon	38
Runny Eggs	42
Hallelujah	48
Edumacation	54
The Lost World	84
Home Again	102
Lunch with Holly	117
It's Black, It's White	125
Merrymaking	135
Otherness	140
Smooth Landing	143
Equality or Not?	150
The Palm	161
What Happened?	164
Hold The Line	169
Cruelty	172
Let's Build Something	176
Unfair	180
Crimson Leaves	184
Irony	188
Numbers Don't Lie	197
Conclusion	227
Acknowledgments	231

Foreword

Why would a former professional basketball star and Hall of Famer write a Forward for a book about a woman musician, lawyer, and U.S. government official? I wrote it because I met Trudi through my wife, Marita, when I played for the New York Knicks more than 50 years ago and I've had the pleasure of observing her character, integrity, and resolve since then.

Her book, *Winning The Battle Against Myself,* traces her childhood with a grandfather who's band included a singer, Hattie McDaniel, her aunt who later won an Oscar for her role in *Gone With the Wind*, and housed famous guests Duke Ellington, Count Basie, William "Bojangles" Robinson, Louis Armstrong, and Nat King Cole, all of whom were barred from Denver hotels because of their race. Trudi's storied career made her the only person of any race or gender to serve in top positions in all three branches of our national government, including the White House, the Senate (where she was one of two people with the authority to arrest the President), and the Judiciary, as the primary trainer of Federal judges in employment dispute resolution.

Winning mirrors my career in several ways. Early on, in the NBA, black players were only allowed to play defense and rebound, the game was geared to white players. The NBA had never seen a black player spin, reverse spin, double pump, deliver deadly jump shots, float, and shoot in mid-air. There was no one I emulated. My only competition was myself. Similarly, the three branches of the U.S. government had

WINNING THE BATTLE AGAINST MYSELF

never seen a black woman with four earned degrees break glass ceilings and fight tirelessly for equality and justice.

Winning describes the encounters Trudi's grandfather had with the Ku Klux Klan in Denver, Colorado. Being black, we've both experienced cabbies refusing to pick us up. My career has been about unpredictability; hers has been about underestimation.

As I developed my style of game, I wasn't taught how to do it. It was all trial and error. When Trudi fought discrimination, misogyny, and hate no one taught her how to do it. It was all instinct and values.

Winning is a must-read for everyone regardless of race, sex, or age. It will inspire you to "never give up."

— Earl "The Pearl" Monroe

Figure 1. -Earl "The Pearl" Monroe with Trudi's Son, Logan (1994).

Introduction

Growing up as a black girl in 1950s America, I was shaped by both the love and perseverance of my family and the harsh realities of a society steeped in racism and misogyny. In this memoir, I trace my journey from a precocious, sickly child to a successful adult striving to break barriers and build on the legacy of excellence modeled by my remarkable forebears. Through my story, I hope to illuminate the challenges and triumphs of coming of age as a black woman in a world that often sought to limit my potential.

Chapter 1

Who Are You? Who Am I?

"Create the highest, grandest vision possible for your life because you become what you believe."
                                            -Oprah Winfrey

Outside the U.S. Capitol building, D.C.'s oppressive summer heat had settled over the city like a wet blanket. The white sandstone exterior glistened in the blinding light. Tourists navigated the streets lined with history, admiring the monuments and oohing and awing over the museums' collections. While inside, I navigated the inner workings of the United States Government.

One day at work, I heard, "Psst! Psst! Girlie! You, Girlie!" My head swiveled, my gaze searching the Senate floor for the voice's intended target. Oh, no! Please don't let him call me.

"Psst! You ... Girlie!" A long, wrinkled, arthritic finger pointed toward me.

My thoughts jumbled and sweat dripped down my spine. One word made its way through the others: Help! He most definitely was talking to me. "Come over here, Girlie." He motioned with a malformed, cupped hand. I approached with enough distance to hear but still far enough back so he couldn't touch me. "Yes, Senator?" My gaze fell to my shoes. I refused to let my fear show. My shoes on the sky-blue carpet calmed me, reminding me of the cloudless sky I'd been admiring that morning on my way to work. "You're not all nigra, are you?"

I couldn't speak. I stared at his head, trying not to let my curiosity show. What are those red dots on his head? Senator Strom Thurmond repeated, "You're not all nigra, are you, Girlie?"

Those red dots, I couldn't stop thinking about them. They were all concentrated near the front of his head. "I can tell by your coloring and hair texture," he continued. "I have to go, Senator," I said. I hurried to the Republican cloakroom, where I could gather myself. When I reached the doorway, I gasped. Senator Barry Goldwater delivered a clenched fist to Senator Ted Stevens' face. An actual fight, right there in the Senate cloakroom. How common. How disgraceful. How trashy.

Two of the most respected men in the United States Senate chose violence to settle a dispute. If they had been black, the outcome would have been much different. Someone would have summoned the Capitol Police to beat them in their heads. After law enforcement barged in, guns blazing, the press corps would have sensationalized photos with clever captions on the front page of every newspaper in the country. Instead, the two senators changed into crisp white shirts and resumed their seats in the chamber without notice. Why did I come to work today?

As I witnessed this astounding scene, my mind flashed back to my earliest memories of the pervasive racism that shaped my world from birth. Even as a child, I was keenly aware of the double standards and barriers that black Americans faced every day. And I knew that my only path forward was to strive for excellence in all things, using my intellect and determination to chip away at the societal limitations placed on me.

Born Premature, Overcoming Challenges

In 1950, baby bottles were made of glass, and not very resilient glass either. My sister Vicki, sixteen months older than me, threw

Who Are You? Who Am I?

one such bottle into my crib one day, narrowly missing my head. Daddy rushed in, scolding Vicki for endangering me. I drifted back to sleep as Vicki, the apple of my parents' eyes, started to cry.

Vicki was a beautiful baby with brown hair and a mocha complexion. As the princess of Paul Quinn College where my father worked, Vicki commanded the adoration of students and starred in campus plays. Pregnant with me, Mommy insisted on returning to St. Luke's Hospital in Denver, where she had given birth to Vicki, rather than face the discriminatory and subpar maternity wards for black women in the South.

I tried to arrive three months early, impatient even before birth. If Mommy hadn't reached Denver in time, neither of us would likely have survived. Daddy had to stay behind in Texas to finish the school year, so Mommy and Vicki made the journey alone. Arriving at barely seven months' gestation, I entered the world fighting for my life.

As a premature baby in 1950, my early months were tenuous. I developed pneumonia and spent weeks in an incubator, my parents waiting anxiously to see if I would pull through. At one point, weighing only 5 pounds 2 ounces, I was so small that my grandfather, George Morrison, Sr., couldn't locate me in the hospital nursery. He rushed to Mommy's room in a panic, only to have her gently explain that I was in the special room for preemies.

Big Daddy, as we called him, was a renowned musician who led an 11-piece jazz orchestra that recorded with Columbia Records. One of the youngest sons of a talented musical family, he started playing violin as a small child, crafting his first instrument out of corn stalks and strings. Despite being a classically trained violinist, he was denied the opportunity to play with major orchestras because of his race. Undeterred, Big Daddy forged his own path, forming bands and delighting audiences across the country with his compositions.

When I was born, Big Daddy was performing at the Annual Cheyenne Frontier Days celebration. He announced my arrival to the crowd, noting that I had the "features of dad and the fixtures of mom." Even in celebrating my birth, he showcased his wit and way with words.

Figure 2. -Big Daddy 1900's.

Figure 3. -Big Daddy and His Orchestra 1920's.

Who Are You? Who Am I?

Battling Illness and Segregation

At the age of four, I found myself once again fighting for my life, this time in an oxygen tent at the Children's Hospital in Denver. I had contracted pneumonia, an illness that was all too common in my early years. As I struggled to breathe and tried to distract myself from the pain, I focused my attention on the duck merry-go-round sent by the mayor, for whom my mother worked as head secretary.

In the bed next to me was a girl named Candy who had long blond hair and seemed to be struggling even more than I was. Her coughing and choking filled me with terror, even as I grappled with my own mortality far too young. When Candy was rushed out of the room surrounded by nurses and doctors, I feared the worst. I never did find out what became of her.

After three harrowing months, I was finally released from the hospital, only to face another challenge soon thereafter. While playing with Vicki, I tripped over the cord of the vaporizer in my room, badly burning my leg with the scalding water and camphor oil. The pain was unbearable, and once again, I was rushed to the hospital.

As I lay in the hospital bed, I overheard the doctor tell my mother that they might need to amputate my badly burned leg. Silently, I prayed with all my might to be spared this fate. Whether through the power of prayer or modern medicine or both, I kept my leg, and today I can hardly see the scars.

These early brushes with death and illness shaped me in profound ways. I learned to be a fighter, to never give up no matter how dire the situation seemed. And I came to understand that as a black child, my life was valued differently by society. The substandard care in segregated hospitals, the dismissive attitudes of some white medical professionals, the lack of resources in black communities - all these factors placed additional barriers in the way of my survival. But I had my family's love and strength behind me, and I was determined to thrive.

WINNING THE BATTLE AGAINST MYSELF

A Complicated Family Legacy

My grandfather, Big Daddy, was a trailblazer in many ways, but his life was also deeply impacted by the racism of the times. In the 1920s, he co-owned a popular jazz club called the Rock Rest Lodge with a Jewish friend. The club attracted top musicians and fans from all over, becoming a cherished gathering place for the black community.

However, their success also drew the ire of the Ku Klux Klan, who threatened to dynamite the club and kill Big Daddy. Fearing for his life and livelihood, he was forced to close the club. This was a devastating blow, but Big Daddy refused to let hate win. He channeled his energies into his music and supporting other black musicians, often hosting famous entertainers like Duke Ellington, Count Basie, William 'Bojangles' Robinson, Louis "Satchmo" Armstrong, and Nat King Cole in his home when they were barred from white hotels.

Figure 4. -Gilpin St. House (Big Momma, Big Daddy, Auntie Marian, and Trudi's Father in front of the house).

Building a home for his family also came with immense challenges in a segregated city. In the 1920s, Big Daddy began construction on a bungalow in a predominantly white neighborhood in Denver. The KKK, which had thousands of members

Who Are You? Who Am I?

in the city, including many prominent officials, tried to stop him at every turn. They destroyed the home's foundation three times during construction. Big Daddy persevered, rebuilding each time until his house was complete.

Even after they moved in, the family faced ongoing attacks and intimidation from the KKK. I vividly remember hearing the stories of Big Daddy rushing out to extinguish a cross burning on their front lawn, neighbors helping to hack it down with axes even as my grandparents comforted their terrified children inside.

The Klan was pervasive in everyday life. The KKK ruled Denver a century ago. Here's how the hate group's legacy is still being felt in 2021: "Klansmen worked at banks, pie companies, railroads, grocery stores, pharmacies, the zoo, the parks, the post office, cab companies, cafes, the stockyard, the city jail, the courthouse, laundry businesses, and this newspaper. They also worked at Denver landmarks, like Elitch Gardens, The Brown Palace Hotel, Union Station, and Lakeside Amusement Park." The Denver Post.

Hate was everywhere, hiding behind every face. Unease reigned. You didn't know who you could trust. The scariest monsters were the ones hiding in plain sight.

But neither the KKK's terror nor the endless indignities of segregation could stop my family from flourishing and finding joy. Mommy's mother, Mama Briggs, had Sunday dinners, where the table overflowed with fried chicken, collard greens, mac and cheese, and her famous lemon meringue pie. The grownups played card games and laughed until tears streamed down their faces, while our cousins, Pat and Nadine staged talent shows and told spooky stories under blanket forts.

Daddy's mother, Big Momma, an artist and beautician, taught me to take pride in my appearance, even when the world tried to tell me that black was not beautiful. She was an expert at pressing hair and mixing up her own cosmetics, passing down wisdom from pioneers like Madame C.J. Walker. But she also encouraged my bookishness, letting me read Reader's Digest magazines under their dining room table.

Figure 5. -Big Momma and Big Daddy (Grandparents - George Sr. and Willa Morrison).

Figure 6. -Mama Briggs, Trudi's Maternal Grandmother.

Hair as Identity and Battleground

As a young black girl in the 1950s, my hair was a constant source of both pride and pain. Wearing it naturally in its

Who Are You? Who Am I?

tightly coiled state was simply not an option in a society that exalted white beauty standards above all else. Mommy spent hours every week hot combing my hair straight, the sizzle of the comb and smell of burning hair a ritual I endured stoically. Lye relaxers were another toxic method used by many black women and girls in that era, a dangerous chemical that could eat through a soda can.

The pressure to have "good hair" - meaning straight, and as close to white texture as possible - was immense. At swimming pools and amusement parks, white attendants would offer Vicki and me scissors to cut off our braids rather than a comb to detangle our chlorine-soaked hair. The implication was clear: our natural hair was unacceptable, something to be ashamed of and erased.

I learned to love my hair pressed and greased into submission, the smell of bergamot and Dixie Peach pomade a comforting scent. But a part of me also longed to break free from the tyranny of the hot comb, to let my coils spring free and frame my face like a halo. It would be decades before the "Black is Beautiful" movement of the 1960s and 70s made this a reality for many black women. And even then, the social and economic costs of embracing natural hair remained high.

Figure 7. -Simone Ross, Trudi's niece.

As an adult, I see my hair as both a battleground and a source of pride, a symbol of my heritage and resilience in the face of oppression. I think of the poetry of Kyle Dargan and his image of a young black boy whose hair is "unkempt and proud," only to have it sheared off into a "black-box history" erasing his true self. I think of my niece Simone; being forced to endure so much hair-based abuse and discrimination.

WINNING THE BATTLE AGAINST MYSELF

Finding Role Models and Inspiration

Growing up, I was fortunate to be surrounded by examples of black excellence in my own family and community. My cousin George, who we affectionately called Georgie, was more like a brother to Vicki and me. A gifted musician with perfect pitch, he could play any song by ear on the piano and had an uncanny knack for making the best sugar cookies.

Georgie's musical talents took him around the world, first as a member of the U.S. Army chorus in Germany, then as a rehearsal pianist with the acclaimed Stuttgart Ballet. Whenever the company performed in the U.S., he would arrange for me to get tickets, treating me to unforgettable performances at the Met in New York City and the Kennedy Center in D.C.

Figure 8. -George Morrison Bailey (cousin).

In my twenties, Georgie arranged for me to see black dancers like Judith Jamison and Arthur Mitchell, who graced those hallowed stages and filled me with pride and a sense of possibility. In the audience, I was often one of a small handful of black faces, keenly aware of the lingering racial divisions in the arts world. But on stage, these artists commanded the space with undeniable skill and presence, their hard-won excellence transcending narrow stereotypes.

Sitting in the plush red velvet seats, I dreamed of a day when black achievement in all fields would be commonplace and unremarkable. A day when little black girls could pursue their passions without constantly having to break down barriers and prove their worth. A day when we would be free to simply be ourselves, without the weight of centuries of oppression on our shoulders.

Coming of Age in Two Worlds

As I grew older, I became increasingly aware of the dual realities I inhabited as a young black woman in America. In my segregated neighborhood and school, I was surrounded by a close-knit village that nurtured my potential and celebrated my accomplishments. The two teachers in my K-12 schooling who looked like me poured knowledge into my eager mind, while neighbors kept watchful eyes on all the children, ready to administer discipline or a hug as needed.

But whenever I ventured into the white world, I was met with icy stares, condescension, and outright hostility. In department stores, saleswomen followed me suspiciously, assuming I was there to steal rather than shop. At the library, I got odd looks from white patrons who seemed surprised to see a black girl browsing the stacks. Even something as simple as trying to catch a taxi could become an ordeal, as drivers routinely passed me by to pick up white customers.

For every instance of racism and rejection, however, there were also moments of connection and hope. Like the elderly white woman who struck up a conversation with me on the bus, insisting that I accept one of her homemade cookies. Or the science teacher who encouraged my love of experiments, slipping me extra books to read on the sly.

At age 35, as I sat in that Senate cloakroom, witnessing the casual brutality and hypocrisy of powerful white men, all these memories washed over me. I thought of my parents and grandparents, who had faced down so much hate and hardship, yet still built lives of dignity and purpose. I thought of Big Daddy, Big Momma, and Mama Briggs, who nurtured my spirit and intellect with music, stories, and unstinting love.

WINNING THE BATTLE AGAINST MYSELF

Most of all, I thought of the little girl I once was, fighting for her life in a hospital bed, unaware of the battles still to come. I whispered a quiet prayer of thanks for her perseverance, her curiosity, her unshakeable belief that she deserved to take up space in this world. And I channeled her spirit as I straightened my spine, lifted my chin, and walked out of that room, determined to keep climbing toward the future she had dared to dream of all those years ago.

Reflection and Next Steps

Revisiting these childhood memories has been a profound and emotional journey. While much has changed since the 1950s, so many of the challenges and indignities I faced as a young black girl remain stubbornly familiar. From microaggressions in the workplace to the ongoing scourge of police violence, the legacy of racism continues to shape every aspect of American life.

Yet I remain hopeful, buoyed by the resilience and ingenuity of my community and the rising generations of young activists who are taking up the mantle of resistance. In telling my story, I hope to add my voice to the chorus calling for change, while also bearing witness to the beauty and brilliance that has always existed within black America.

As I continue working on this memoir, I plan to dive even deeper into the events and experiences that shaped my path from childhood to the halls of power. I want to explore the intersections of race, gender, and class that have defined my life, and grapple with the ways in which my own privilege and success have sometimes shielded me from the harsher realities faced by so many in my community.

Most of all, I want to celebrate the unsung heroes who have lifted me up and inspired me along the way - the teachers and mentors, the artists and activists, the neighbors and friends

Who Are You? Who Am I?

who have been my village. For it is only by remembering and honoring our shared history that we can begin to imagine a brighter future for us all.

Chapter 2

School Daze

*"Women are always saying, 'We can do anything that men can do.'
But men should be saying, 'We can do anything that women can do.'"*
-Gloria Steinem

As a young girl growing up in the 1950s Denver, this sentiment would have seemed radical, almost unthinkable. The world I inhabited was one strictly divided along lines of race and gender, where expectations and opportunities were determined by the color of your skin and the shape of your body. But even then, I had an unshakeable sense that something about this was fundamentally wrong - a sense that would grow into a lifelong commitment to fighting injustice wherever I found it.

Much of this conviction came from my parents, who each taught me to stand up for myself and for what was right. My father, George Morrison, Jr., was a towering figure in my life, a respected educator who believed fiercely in the power of knowledge and hard work to overcome any obstacle.

I remember one day in second grade, after I won the election for student body president, the principal told me I was too young for the responsibility and that a sixth grade boy who came in second would take over the role. When Daddy found out about the principal's decision he sat me down and looked me straight in the eye. "Trudi Michelle, you can do anything you set your mind to," he said firmly. "Don't let anyone tell you differently, not because you're a girl or because you're Negro or because you're not the right age, you hear me?"

I did hear him, loud and clear. And I carried those words with me like a talisman as I navigated the treacherous terrain of a predominantly white elementary school. Daddy taught me to hold my head high in the face of the daily slights and humiliations to channel my anger into excellence and achievement.

Figure 9. -Marjorie and George Morrison & children Vicki and Trudi, 1951.

When I came home from school with torn dresses and scraped knees from yet another schoolyard scuffle, Mommy would clean my wounds and remind me I had a choice in how to fight back. Mama Briggs would tell me to "Use your mind, not just your fists," tapping my forehead gently. "That's where your real power lies."

WINNING THE BATTLE AGAINST MYSELF

But while Daddy emphasized individual strength and perseverance, my mother Marjorie taught me the importance of collective action in the face of systemic oppression. In 1958, when she set out to buy our family's first home in the nearly all-white neighborhood of Park Hill, Mommy knew she was waging a battle much larger than herself.

At the time, discriminatory practices like redlining and racially restrictive covenants made it nearly impossible for black families to secure housing outside of designated areas. Banks routinely denied loans to qualified black buyers, and real estate agents steered them away from white neighborhoods with dire warnings of plummeting property values and white flight.

But Mommy was undeterred. Armed with meticulous research and an unwavering sense of purpose, she confronted the bank officials who tried to deny our loan application, citing bogus concerns about our family's "financial stability." She organized with other black homebuyers to pressure the city council and mayor's office to investigate discriminatory lending practices. And when we finally moved into our new house on Cherry Street, she formed a neighborhood committee to welcome other black families and promote integration.

I watched in awe as Mommy stared down the men in suits who sought to keep us in our place, never once lowering her gaze or backing down from her convictions. From her, I learned that change was possible, but it required organization, strategy, and an unflinching commitment to justice.

These early lessons would be put to the test again and again as I navigated the ups and downs of childhood and adolescence. Whether I was facing down bullies in the schoolyard or organizing impromptu civil rights brown bag lunches with my sister Vicki and our best friend Charlayne, I drew strength from my parent's example and the knowledge that I was part of a larger struggle.

One of my most vivid memories from this time was the day in 1963 when Vicki and I convinced Charlayne to join us in integrating the whites-only public swimming pool at Congress

School Daze

Park. It was a sweltering summer afternoon, and the three of us had been biking around the neighborhood, working up a sweat and a thirst for adventure.

When we arrived at the pool, the attendant, a freckle-faced teenager with a whistle around his neck, looked at us like we had two heads. "Sorry, no Coloreds allowed," he said, crossing his arms over his skinny chest.

But we had come too far to be dissuaded by a pimply kid. I, always the ringleader, marched right up to him and looked him dead in the eye. "That's unconstitutional," I said calmly. "The Supreme Court said so in Brown v. Board of Education. You have to let us in."

The attendant's mouth opened and closed like a goldfish, but no words came out. He looked around nervously, as if hoping someone else would intervene and save him from this unexpected civics lesson. But I pressed on, my voice rising with righteous indignation.

"If you don't let us in, we'll have no choice but to file a formal complaint with the city," I continued. "And I'm sure the newspapers would be very interested to hear about how the parks department is flouting the law and discriminating against Negro kids. Plus, our mom works for the mayor."

By now, a small crowd had gathered around us, drawn by the commotion. Some looked amused, others irritated, but no one stepped forward to challenge my arguments. Finally, with a sigh of resignation, the attendant unhooked the chain from the gate and waved us through.

"Fine, go ahead," he muttered. "But if anyone asks, I never saw you."

We marched past him with our heads held high, trying to ignore the stares and whispers of the white sunbathers who clearly hadn't expected to be sharing their leisure time with a trio of black girls. But as we laid out our towels and surveyed the sparkling blue water before us, I felt a surge of pride and happiness that no amount of sideways glances could dampen.

WINNING THE BATTLE AGAINST MYSELF

That day at the pool was a small victory in the grand scheme of things, but it felt momentous to me. It was a reminder that the world was changing, slowly but surely, and that we had the power to nudge it along with acts of courage and defiance. And it was a testament to the unbreakable bond of sisterhood that Vicki, Charlayne and I had forged, a bond that would sustain us through the challenges and triumphs to come.

Figure 10. -Vicki (2) and Trudi (10 mo.), 1951.

***

That bond was tested at times, of course, like the time Vicki convinced me to let her put on a tourniquet and cut my leg to get bacon. Don't ask me why, but somehow, I trusted my big sister when she said it was the only way. Blood gushed from my swollen leg, which had turned blue - the same leg I had scalded as a child.

The babysitter ran out of the room, returned with a kitchen knife, and cut the cloth off my knee. Unfortunately, her panic and the swelling caused the babysitter to dig deep into the inside of my knee with the knife. I carry that scar to this day. It was a silly, reckless moment, but it spoke to the depths of our trust and the lengths we would go to for each other, even if it meant a little pain and a lasting scar.

On warm summer evenings, we played four square in Charlayne's driveway. The white house next to Charlayne was the only house on the block that was painted instead of brick, set farther back with a driveway leading to a three-car garage in front. Most kids avoided the house at Halloween, but my curiosity got the best of me one year.

"C'mon on, Vicki. What could happen with all these kids and parents around?" I argued in my pumpkin costume.

"Are you kidding? There are no lights on," Vicki, the Halloween witch said, her hat tipping too far left. I balled up more newspapers to stuff in it.

"Well, I'm going up there anyway."

Vicki straightened her hat and followed me.

The dark outside helped us see inside the lighted house. On the center table, a smoking black cauldron was surrounded by dancing paper ghosts. We counted six dangling skeletons, nine scary carved pumpkins, and fifteen bumpy gourds. Flying bats and grinning black cats with orange eyes glared back at us as green slime oozed down the walls.

I reached for Vicki's hand, but she was gone. When did she leave? Where did she go? Suddenly, a man appeared with loaded trays of orange and black frosted cupcakes. Others brought candy corn, dishes, sandwiches, candied apples, cotton candy, punch, brownies, chips and pretzels galore. Two miserable costumed dogs meandered by.

A hand touched my shoulder. I was sure it was the hand of death.

"I saw you at the window, so I brought you a plate of goodies. Here are your Halloween treats," the hand of death said.

"Thank you," I whispered, running home as fast as I could. Vicki was watching TV.

"Where did you go? Why did you leave me?"

"I didn't leave you. I just came home."

WINNING THE BATTLE AGAINST MYSELF

"Look." I showed her the plate of snacks.

"Wow. Those look yummy." Then she threw the plate of goodies from the white house of Horror in the trash.

"What are you doing? Why did you do that?"

"Trudi, you remember Hansel and Gretel, don't you?" We never spoke of it again.

***

As I looked back on those early years, I realized how much my childhood had been shaped by the interlocking forces of racism, sexism, and resistance. From the redlined neighborhoods and segregated schools to the daily indignities of being judged by the color of my skin, I had learned to navigate a world that was stacked against me in countless ways.

But I had also learned that I was not alone in this struggle. I had my parents, my sister, my friends and neighbors all fighting alongside me in ways big and small. And I had the growing realization that the very things that made me a target - my race, my gender, my uncompromising sense of justice - were also the sources of my strength and resilience.

As I prepared to leave for college and embark on the next chapter of my journey, I knew I was ready for whatever challenges lay ahead. I had been forged in the crucible of the civil rights movement, tempered by the love and wisdom of my family and community. And I was determined to use my voice and my talents to continue the work of bending the arc of the moral universe toward justice, no matter where that path might lead me.

Little did I know then just how far that path would take me - from the streets of Denver to the halls of power in Washington D.C. and beyond. But as I looked to the future with a mix of excitement and trepidation, I knew one thing for certain: I would never stop fighting for what was right, no matter how daunting the odds or how fierce the opposition.

School Daze

With a heart full of hope and a mind sharpened by adversity, I stepped out into the world, ready to take my place in the long line of freedom fighters who had come before me. The road ahead would be long and winding, but I knew I had the strength and the conviction to see it through to the end.

Chapter 3

Oozing Cakes

"Let them eat cake."

— Marie Antoinette

The irony of that infamous quote was not lost on me as I watched Mrs. Moore, one of the stalwart church ladies of Shorter A.M.E Church, carefully scraping peas and rolls off used plates and arranging them on fresh ones to serve to unsuspecting guests. It was a small deception, perhaps, in the grand scheme of things - but it felt emblematic of the larger hypocrisies and contradictions I would come to see in the institution that had once been the center of my family's life.

Growing up in the 1950s and 60s, the church was everything to us. Shorter A.M.E Church, with its stately brick edifice and soaring sanctuary, was not just a place of worship but the beating heart of Denver's black community. It was where we went to sing and pray, to gossip and flirt, to celebrate and mourn and everything in between.

As children, Vicki and I were there almost every day of the week, it seemed. Sundays for services, of course, but also Wednesdays for choir practice, Tuesdays for Bible study, Thursdays for youth groups. We had picnics and plays, skating parties and

Oozing Cakes

bake sales. The older boys played basketball in the gymnasium while the girls huddled in the corner, pretending not to watch.

It was a busy, boisterous world, full of laughter and drama and intrigue. But even as a young girl, I couldn't help but notice the small cracks in the facade - the little ways in which the piety and propriety of Sunday morning gave way to the messy realities of human nature.

There was Mrs. Moore with her recycled peas, of course, and the sad, soggy pound cakes that oozed raw batter when my mother cut into them before a bake sale. There were the whispered rumors about this deacon or that choir director, the sideways glances and snickers behind gloved hands.

And then there was the politics. As I got older, I began to notice how the pastor would drop not-so-subtle hints about which candidates the congregation should support, or rail against this or that piece of legislation from the pulpit. It made me uncomfortable, even then - the idea that the church could be used as a tool for earthly power rather than a sanctuary for the soul.

But mostly, I remember the sense of community that permeated every aspect of church life. The way the mothers of the church would press a peppermint into your hand if you started to nod off during a particularly long-winded sermon. The deep, rumbling harmonies of the men's choir that seemed to make the very walls vibrate. The feeling of belonging to something bigger than yourself, of being part of a rich and sacred tradition.

As I grew older, though, that sense of belonging began to fray. I found myself chafing at the strictures and expectations of the church, the pressure to conform to a narrow vision of what it meant to be a good Christian woman. I bristled at the judgmental whispers and sidelong glances when I dared to question a point of doctrine or challenge a decision by the leadership.

Slowly but surely, I pulled away. I would slip out of the sanctuary during particularly political sermons, claiming a headache or a forgotten task. I stopped volunteering for

WINNING THE BATTLE AGAINST MYSELF

committees and bake sales, stopped attending youth groups and Tuesday night Bible study.

By the time I left for college, my disillusionment was complete. The church, which had once been the center of my world, now felt small and stifling - a place of hypocrisy and contradiction rather than love and liberation.

Looking back now, I can see that my experiences in the church were a microcosm of the larger struggles I would face as a black woman in America. The pressure to conform, to keep up appearances, to shrink myself to fit into the narrow boxes that society had prescribed for me - these were battles I would fight again and again, in every aspect of my life.

But I also knew that the church had given me something valuable, something that I would carry with me always. It had given me a sense of my worth and dignity, a belief in the power of community and the importance of standing up for what was right. It had given me my voice.

And so, even as I left the physical building of Shorter A.M.E Church behind, I carried its lessons with me. I carried the memory of my mother, staying up all night to bake cakes from scratch so that her children would never be associated with anything less than excellence. I carried the wisdom of the old folks who had seen so much hardship and yet still found reason to praise and give thanks. I carried the fierce, unbending faith of my ancestors, who had built the church and used it as a bulwark against the cruelties of the world and a force for change and justice.

As I stepped out into the wider world, I knew I would need every ounce of that faith and that strength. I knew that the road ahead would be long and hard, that there would be setbacks and disappointments and moments of despair. But I also knew that I was not alone - that I was part of a lineage of resistance and resilience that stretched back generations and would carry me forward, no matter what challenges lay ahead.

Oozing Cakes

And so, with a heart full of hope and a spirit forged in the fire of the church, I set out to make my mark on the world - to fight for justice, to speak truth to power, and to build a life of purpose and meaning. The journey ahead would be long, but I was ready for it. I had been preparing my whole life.

Chapter 4

Brown Sugar and Cinnamon

> "I never had anything good, no sweet, no sugar; and that sugar, right by me, did look so nice, and my mistress's back was turned to me while she was fighting with her husband, so I just put my fingers in the sugar bowl to take one lump, and maybe she heard me, for she turned and saw me. The next minute, she had the rawhide down."
>
> -Harriet Tubman

The smell of cinnamon and brown sugar, warm and sweet, drifting down the stairs to wake us on Christmas morning. That's what I remember most about the holidays as a child - not the presents or the twinkling lights (though there were plenty of those), but the sense of comfort and anticipation that filled our house like a gentle fog.

I would lie in bed, listening to the clatter of pots and pans from the kitchen above, knowing that my mother was already hard at work on her famous cinnamon buns. They were a once-a-year treat, reserved for Christmas morning, and the mere thought of them was enough to send Vicki and me racing upstairs in our pajamas, giddy with excitement.

We would find my mother in the kitchen, her hair pulled back in a neat bun, her apron dusted with flour. She would shoo us away with a smile, telling us to be patient, that the buns weren't ready yet. But she always let us help with the final step - spreading the soft dough with butter and showering it with cinnamon and brown sugar until it was glistening and fragrant.

As we worked, my mother would tell us stories about the long history of Negro cooks and the impact they had on American cuisine. She told us about the enslaved chefs who became renowned for their skills in the plantation kitchens of the South, and the black women who later found work as cooks and housekeepers in the homes of white families.

One of those women was my grandmother, Cora Briggs, who worked as a cook at a boarding house in Denver called Charmwood. In 1954, she even appeared in an issue of Life Magazine, pictured next to a table laden with lemon pies and hams and turkeys. Mama Briggs was a fixture in our family's culinary history, passing down recipes and traditions that had been handed down for generations.

As I grew older, I understood the deeper significance of those traditions - the way that food and cooking could be a source of pride and resistance in the face of oppression. I thought of Harriet Tubman's words, describing the small, subversive act of stealing a lump of sugar from her mistress's bowl. In a world that denied black people even the most basic pleasures and comforts, the kitchen could be a place of power and defiance.

But in my childhood, those weighty considerations were far from my mind. Christmas was a time of pure, unfettered joy - a time when the hardships and injustices of the outside world seemed to melt away like the brown sugar in my mother's buns.

There were the Christmas carols Big Daddy would lead us in singing as we tramped through the snowy streets of Denver, his rich baritone voice ringing out above the rest. There were the piles of presents that seemed to multiply every year, the shiny bicycles and baby dolls that filled our living room to bursting. The only downside was Mommy's insistence that we put the delicate icicles back in the box they came out of. Due to their fragile, thin composition, most of them broke anyway.

WINNING THE BATTLE AGAINST MYSELF

And then there was Big Daddy himself, his booming laugh and twinkling eyes the very embodiment of Christmas cheer. I'll never forget the year Daddy and Big Daddy rode our bikes through the park from Big Daddy's house to our house. Big Daddy, Denver's Godfather of Jazz, rode my new bicycle straight into a tree, denting the fender. Daddy told us that Big Daddy spent all night trying to hammer out the damage, grumbling good-naturedly.

But even Big Daddy's antics couldn't dampen the magic of those Christmas mornings. As we sat around the table, devouring the cinnamon buns and sipping hot cocoa, everything felt right in the world. We were safe and loved and together, and for a moment, that was enough.

Looking back now, I understand how much effort and care went into creating those perfect moments. I think about my mother, rising before dawn to knead the dough and letting us "help" even though we probably made a mess. I think about my father, teetering on a ladder to string the lights just right, my grandmother laboring over a hot stove to make sure everyone had their fill, and family members serenading us with musical love.

I think, too, about the sacrifices and struggles that made those moments possible - the discrimination and hardship that my parents and grandparents faced every day, the strength and resilience that allowed them to create a sense of warmth and security for us even in the face of so much adversity.

Those Christmas memories, glowing and golden in my mind, were a testament to the power of family and the unbreakable bonds of love. They were a reminder that even in the darkest of times, there could be light and laughter and the sweet smell of cinnamon.

As I grew older and began to face my own challenges and struggles, I would often think back to those mornings around the kitchen table, to the feeling of being surrounded by the people who loved me most in the world. And I would draw strength from the knowledge that I carried that love with me always, a flame that could never be extinguished no matter how hard the world might try.

So, when I smell cinnamon now, it's not just the ghost of Christmas past that comes rushing back to me. It's the spirit of my family, the legacy of resilience and joy that has sustained us through generations of hardship and triumph. It's the reminder that no matter what challenges we may face, we will always have each other - and that is a gift more precious than any shiny bicycle or baby doll.

As I reflect on those long-ago Christmases, I am filled with gratitude for the love and laughter that filled my childhood home. And I am more determined than ever to carry on the traditions and values that have been passed down to me - to create a life that honors the sacrifices of my ancestors and paves the way for a brighter future for generations to come.

Because in the end, that is the true meaning of Christmas - not the presents or the feasts, but the enduring power of family and the unshakeable bonds of love. It is the knowledge that no matter what the world may bring, we will always have a place to call home, a warm kitchen to return to, and the sweet smell of cinnamon to guide us there.

Figure 11. -Trudi's Parents (Marjorie and George), 1987.

Chapter 5

Runny Eggs

"Gentleness doesn't get work done unless you happen to be a hen laying eggs."

-Coco Chanel

"Can I help dye the eggs, Daddy?" I asked, my eyes wide with anticipation.

"Of course. That's yours and Vicki's job," Daddy replied with a smile.

He put a towel in a deep pan, placed the pan under the faucet, and filled it with cold water. Daddy asked Vicki to grab the cartons of eggs from the refrigerator. People told us we had eggs at Easter because giving eggs celebrated a new life. The eggshell represented Christ's tomb, while the chick represented Jesus.

After the eggs were boiled, Daddy said, "Get the ice trays out, girls, and the large crock bowl." We ran into each other, rushing around our tiny kitchen. Daddy got the ice from the stainless-steel ice trays by pulling the lever on the tray. He filled the bowl with ice and cold water.

It seemed like forever waiting for the eggs to cool. While they cooled, I got four bowls out of the cabinet and opened the egg dye kit. Vicki put red, yellow, green, and blue food colors

Runny Eggs

in each bowl. Daddy poured vinegar into the bowls. Vicki and I pinched our noses and laughed at the stink.

"Why do the eggs need vinegar?" I asked.

"Vinegar helps the coloring stick to the egg and makes the color more vibrant. Be careful with the eggs, Pumpkin Head," Daddy replied.

"I will," Vicki said.

Pumpkin Head was Daddy's nickname for Vicki. We didn't know why. Her head didn't look like a pumpkin to me. My nickname was Beaver.

"Why do you call me Beaver, Daddy?" I asked.

"Because you chew on your knotty pine bed. Look at it. The headboard has your teeth marks all over it," he explained.

I was quiet. I knew my headboard had bite marks everywhere. Mommy told me I was born with a nervous tick. Maybe my chewing on wood was related to early anxiety.

"Did you know that beavers are intelligent, gentle, reasoning beings who enjoy playing practical jokes?" Daddy asked.

"No, I didn't know that. But I'm glad that beavers are smart!" I said with pride.

"Concentrate, Trudi Babe. Turn the eggs. You want to make the color on the egg as even as possible," Daddy instructed.

"Oh, no, this side is really dark purple. I should've turned it sooner, Daddy. I ruined it," I lamented.

"No, you didn't ruin it. It's the prettiest one we've made. It's two-toned!" Daddy reassured me.

I beamed with delight. Mommy came into the kitchen with something in her hand.

"I found these patterned napkins that may give you all some ideas for decorating the eggs," she said.

I was surprised that Mommy was interested in what we were doing. Egg decorating was what Daddy did with us.

"How cool, Mommy. We learned something in Art class I'd like to try," Vicki said.

"Just don't make a mess," Mommy cautioned.

WINNING THE BATTLE AGAINST MYSELF

Vicki rolled her eyes and ran downstairs. She came back with a bottle in her hand.

"What's that?" I asked, pointing to her hand.

"It's a glossy decoupage lacquer to put on the back of the paper. Then we can cover the whole egg with paper and brush decoupage lacquer on top. The paper will get tighter when it dries," Vicki explained.

Vicki always came up with creative and goofy ideas. I didn't know which one this was.

"What did you say? What are you talking about doing to the eggs?" I asked, confused.

"Decoupage is using cutouts from magazines or other paper and gluing them to the eggs and coating the cutouts with lacquer," she clarified.

"That sounds hard. Can I try?"

"Sure. Go get a small paintbrush so we can get started," Vicki said.

I dashed downstairs and collected different-sized brushes from my wooden storage case. Back in the kitchen, I held them up. "Which size do we use?"

"A bigger one for the lacquer and smaller ones to press the paper onto the eggs," Vicki instructed.

I started putting the glue on an egg but pressed too hard, and the egg cracked. I shrieked.

Mommy rushed into the kitchen. "What happened?" she asked.

"An egg cracked, that's all, Marj," Daddy said.

Mommy hugged me. We finished decorating the eggs and refrigerated them.

Mommy still had to wash and press our hair. That took a couple of hours. I dreaded it.

"Trudi — your turn," Mommy said.

Sigh. There was no escape. "Here I come."

Mommy placed a towel around my shoulders and parted my slightly damp hair into four sections. She moisturized my

Runny Eggs

hair first. Then she tested the temperature of the hot comb, which was heated by flame on the gas stove, by putting spit on her finger and touching the hot comb. The comb sizzled. It was ready. She pulled slowly from the root to the top of the strands with the hot comb. I sat in the steamy kitchen for hours, dodging the fiery instrument and getting nicked on the ear and neck by the hot comb. My hair, face, and neck were greasy for days.

She bought us new outfits, including shoes, purses, and hats. In the morning, we went to church in our new Easter outfits to celebrate the life of Jesus Christ. We got eggs at church, but they weren't cooked through. They broke and smeared inside my new Easter purse during the church service.

I held my open purse toward my sister. "Vicki, look! Those eggs broke and yellow yolks have ruined my new purse." My eyes started watering.

"The same thing happened to my purse, Trudi. Let's tell Mommy and Daddy," Vicki said.

Mommy told me to speak quietly and that we would talk about the eggs later.

After church, we got together with friends and family for a special meal and an Easter egg scavenger hunt. We ate ham, pot roast, macaroni and cheese, collard greens, rolls, potato salad, and marshmallow-topped sweet potatoes. Vicki, my friends, and I crawled around the yard, looking for hidden treasures. We found eggs the Easter Bunny hid on low branches and in open places. I carried a basket to collect as many of these treats as possible. I didn't find many eggs, but the kids got prizes in exchange for each egg at the end of the hunt. Mommy and Daddy told me that there were prizes left that Vicki and I would get that evening.

Later Easter night, Mommy said, "That church gives you kids undercooked eggs every year. I'm going to speak to the pastor about this. Haven't they heard of Salmonella?"

"What's Samoyellow?" I asked.

"Sal - mon - ella," Mommy said.

WINNING THE BATTLE AGAINST MYSELF

"Salmonella are bacteria in your tummy that can give you diarrhea and pain. You can't smell it or taste it, but it makes you very sick."

"I'm not eating eggs anymore," Vicki said.

"But I like eggs, Mommy. Why can't we eat them anymore?" I asked.

"Of course, we'll eat eggs, Trudi. Vicki said that because I told you kids about the bad bacteria that can get into eggs if they aren't taken care of properly. But I always make sure to store and prepare them, so we don't get sick," Mommy explained.

"I'm glad you do that," I said.

"Me, too," Vicki agreed.

With Mommy taking care of the dyed eggs for us, we had no worries. She was always prepared and thought of everything. Mommy would let us eat two eggs on Easter Sunday. The remaining eggs would appear as egg salad, deviled eggs, ham hash with eggs and mustard sauce, open-faced shrimp, tomato, lemon, and egg sandwiches, and other mystery egg concoctions.

As I reflect on those Easter memories, I am reminded of the love and care that went into every tradition, no matter how small or imperfect. The runny eggs, the messy decorating, the hair-pressing ordeals - they were all part of the tapestry of our family life, woven together with laughter, tears, and an unshakeable bond of love.

Those traditions shaped me in ways I am still discovering, teaching me the value of perseverance, creativity, and finding beauty in the flaws. They showed me that even in a world that often seeks to diminish and devalue black women, there is strength and resilience to be found in the simple act of coming together and celebrating our unique heritage.

And so, as I navigate the challenges and triumphs of my adult life, I carry those Easter lessons with me, a reminder of the power of family, faith, and the unbreakable spirit that has carried my people through generations of struggle and triumph. Those runny eggs, it turns out, were not just a messy inconvenience

Runny Eggs

- they were a symbol of the imperfect beauty and boundless love that have shaped me into the woman I am today.

Figure 12. -Trudi and her Mother, Marjorie, January, 1985.

Figure 13. -Trudi's Sister Vicki, April, 1994.

Chapter 6

Hallelujah

"The arts and sciences are avatars of human creativity."
Mae Jemison

The first time I played the Hallelujah Chorus from Handel's Messiah, I felt something shift inside me. It was like a door opening to a new world, one where beauty and meaning transcended the limits of everyday life.

I was sixteen years old, sitting in the string section of the Shorter A.M.E Church orchestra, my fingers flying over the strings of my beloved upright bass. Next to me was my cousin Georgie, his brow furrowed in concentration as he coaxed the low notes from his own instrument. In front of us, my father and grandfather stood side by side, their violins raised in perfect unison, while my Auntie Marian's fingers danced over the keys of the piano.

As the chorus swelled around us, I felt a rush of joy and connection that I had never experienced before. The music seemed to fill every corner of the church, lifting us all up with its message of hope and redemption.

In that moment, I understood the true power of art - its ability to unite people across boundaries of race, class, and creed, to speak to our deepest hopes and fears, to make us feel like we were part of something greater than ourselves.

That feeling of transcendence was one I had been chasing ever since I first picked up an instrument at the age of four. Growing up in a family of musicians, music was as much a part of my life as breathing. I started with the piano, spending hours every day practicing scales and arpeggios under the watchful eye of my Auntie Marian. Later, I picked up the bass, drawn to its deep, resonant tones and the way it anchored the sound of any ensemble.

Figure 14. -Auntie Marian (Georgie's Mother, Daddy's Sister), 1997.

But mastering these instruments was never easy for me. I had physical differences in both hands from incidents in my youth - a steel door slammed down on my left pinky finger at one of Daddy's jobs, and my sister hit my right hand too hard, recessing the knuckle into a disability while we were playing a card game called 'knuckles.'

I had to work twice as hard as other students to make my fingers obey my commands. I spent long hours in the practice room, fighting through the pain and frustration, determined to prove that I could be just as skilled as anyone else.

WINNING THE BATTLE AGAINST MYSELF

In some ways, this determination reflected the broader challenges I faced as a young black girl growing up in the 1960s. Everywhere I looked, it seemed, there were barriers and obstacles - from the segregated schools and neighborhoods of my childhood to the subtle and not-so-subtle forms of racism and sexism I encountered as I grew older.

But I was lucky to have parents who taught me to confront these challenges head-on, to use my intellect and my talents to fight for what was right. I'll never forget the conversation we had when I was twelve years old, about the history of slavery and the compromises that had shaped our nation's founding documents.

"Trudi Babe, you have to understand," my father said, his voice firm but gentle. "The framers of the Constitution were men of their time. They made compromises, yes - but they also laid the groundwork for a system that could evolve and change over time."

My mother nodded in agreement, her eyes flashing with a mix of anger and determination. "And it's up to us to keep pushing that change forward," she said. "To fight for a world where everyone is truly equal, no matter the color of their skin or the shape of their bodies."

I took their words to heart, diving into my studies with renewed determination. When I started junior high, I was thrilled to have my first black teacher, Mr. Blanton. He was a brilliant science teacher who pushed us to think critically and dream big. For me, he was more than just a role model - he was proof that intelligence and excellence knew no color, and that I could achieve anything I set my mind to. Plus, I had a crush on him until I saw him kiss a woman who dropped him off in front of the school. I wanted to be his wife, not her. At that moment, I decided to give up on men.

Disillusioned, I threw myself into extracurricular activities, joining the student council and running for president. I'll never forget the thrill of victory when I won that election - the sense of pride and possibility that came with knowing I had earned the trust and respect of my peers.

But even as I excelled academically, music remained my true passion. I continued to study piano and bass, spending hours practicing my favorite pieces - from Beethoven's Fur Elise to Gershwin's Rhapsody in Blue. And when I was selected each year for the All-City and All-State Orchestras, I knew that all my hard work had paid off.

It was through these musical experiences that I met Eugene Fodor, the violin prodigy who would become one of my closest friends and fiercest competitors. Gene was a true virtuoso, with a gift for coaxing impossible sounds from his instrument. I'll never forget the first time I heard him play - the way his fingers danced across the strings, the raw emotion that poured out of every note.

"I've never heard that kind of musicianship, Gene," I told him after one particularly stunning performance.

He just shrugged nonchalantly, as if it were no big deal. "I'm pretty good at it," he said with a grin. "Relaxation of my wrist is the key."

"How long do you practice each day?" I asked, already knowing the answer would put my dedication to shame.

"Between six and eight hours," he replied casually.

My eyes widened in amazement. "Far out! You are incredible."

And he was - in more ways than one. Gene made his solo debut with the Denver Symphony Orchestra at age ten and began touring internationally at twelve. In 1974, he became the first American violinist to win top honors at the prestigious International Tchaikovsky Competition in Moscow.

But for all his success, I knew that Gene's path had not been an easy one. He had grown up with an abusive father who pushed him relentlessly, and the pressure to be perfect had taken a toll on his mental health. Even as he dazzled audiences around the world, I could see the cracks starting to show - the late nights, the mood swings, the growing reliance on alcohol and drugs to cope with the stress.

I did my best to be there for him, to offer a listening ear and a shoulder to cry on. But in the end, I knew that Gene's demons were too powerful for anyone else to slay. When he was kicked out of Jascha Heifetz's elite violin studio at USC for performing without the wig that covered his long hair, it felt like the beginning of the end.

Still, I never could have imagined the tragic news that would reach me years later - that Gene had died alone in a hotel room at the age of 60, his once-brilliant mind and body ravaged by addiction. It was a loss that shook me to my core, a stark reminder of the fragility of even the most prodigious talent.

But even in my grief, I knew that Gene's legacy would live on - not just in the recordings and memories he left behind, but in the lessons he had taught me about the power and the price of pursuing one's passions to the fullest.

As I look back on those formative years now, I see how much they shaped the person I would become. The work ethic and determination I learned from my parents, the sense of possibility and pride I gained from teachers like Mr. Blanton, the joy and camaraderie I found in music - all of these would serve as a foundation for the challenges and triumphs that lay ahead.

And at the center of it all was that unshakeable belief in the transformative power of art - the conviction that music, in all its beauty and complexity, had the ability to change lives, to bring people together, to make the world a bit brighter and more bearable.

It was a belief that would sustain me through the darkest times, through the long nights of practice, and the lonely moments of self-doubt. And it was a belief that would inspire me to keep pushing forward, to use my talents and my platform to fight for the causes I believed in.

Because in the end, I knew that my purpose was about more than just making beautiful sounds. It was about using

Hallelujah

my voice to speak truth to power, to shine a light on injustice and inequality wherever I found it. It was about being a force for change and progress, even when the odds seemed impossibly stacked against me.

And so, I kept playing, kept fighting, kept believing - secure in the knowledge that I was part of a proud lineage of artists and activists who had come before me, and that my own contributions, however small, would help to carry that legacy forward.

As I stood on that stage in church, feeling the power of the Hallelujah Chorus coursing through my veins, I felt a sense of gratitude and purpose that I knew would stay with me forever. This was what I was meant to do, who I was meant to be. And nothing - not the limitations of my body, not the prejudices of society, not the obstacles that lay ahead - could ever take that away from me.

I was Trudi Morrison - musician, activist, dreamer, and fighter. And I was just getting started.

Figure 15. -Big Daddy on violin, Auntie Marian on piano, Aunt Hattie (Hattie McDaniel) seated and Big Momma standing, 1948.

Chapter 7

Edumacation

"You have to stay in school. You have to. You have to go to college. You have to get your degree. Because that's the one thing people can't take away from you is your education. And it is worth the investment."
                                                            -Michelle Obama

During summers, I was a Candy Striper at Rose Hospital. I wore a pink and white striped pinafore with a crisp white blouse. I only had one uniform, so I'd wash it, starch the blouse, and iron it every night. And every morning, I'd ride the Colorado Boulevard bus #40 south to the hospital. I wanted to help others and give back. My family was a caring family that donated time and money to needy people. It was time to step up and do my part. I made a list of all the ways I was blessed. I put my blessings in alphabetical order to remember them all. For instance, under "B," I listed my bass violin; under "H," I helped an elderly church member; under "P," I put a piano. God had given me so much; it was my duty to give something to others.

As soon as I arrived at Rose Hospital, I supported the nurses by making beds, refilling water and ice, assisting nurses by taking vital signs, changing linens, emptying trash, delivering flowers, restocking supplies, cleaning rooms, carrying books and magazines to rooms, and reading to the patients.

Edumacation

The volunteer work taught me a lot about myself. One resounding lesson was to be patient with myself and take time to figure out my future goals. I knew I had something to offer the world and that finding my purpose would take time. It made me understand that comforting others also comforted me.

As a Candy Striper, I was able to help older adults sleep better and express themselves more. For example, a former teacher was hospitalized with a stroke that paralyzed her arm and leg. Her mind was still strong, though. The more I read to her, the more she responded with her memories of reading to her classes. Soon, she started reading to me! The nurses told me I helped her recover by giving her a sense of purpose. By reading to me, she knew she was still valued. I could also recognize how vital volunteering was. It filled a gap in patient care.

Some patients were lonely and scared, and my presence reassured and cheered them. I learned that it's easy to walk into a hospital and feel depressed about the lack of mobility and energy. What is missed in older patients are the years of experience, the wisdom, and the need to contribute—to be involved.

Daddy was a stickler for healthy feet. He bought us Buster Brown shoes and high-top Converse tennis shoes. The fact that he was a coach didn't help our position that we hated the high tops. Daddy told us that high-top sneakers helped minimize the risk of spraining our ankles. I didn't completely understand.

"Daddy, how can a piece of cloth stand up against my body weight?"

"It will help but not stop you from an ankle sprain," Daddy explained.

"Have you ever sprained your ankle?"

"Three or four times. Coaching is hard on the ankles and knees."

"Is that why you have all those ACE bandages in the drawer?"

"Yes, they help reduce swelling and pain if wrapped the right way. Wrapping helps the injury heal and might prevent you from hurting it again."

WINNING THE BATTLE AGAINST MYSELF

"That makes sense."

Our conversation ended. Our Buster Browns were polished and shined every morning and sat by our bedroom door.

We brought our gym clothes home to wash every Friday. One weekend, Vicki had an idea.

"Go get a pair of scissors from the upstairs kitchen drawer," Vicki said. There were two kitchens in our house.

Uh-oh, is this gonna be another of Vicki's kooky ideas?

"What are we gonna do, Vicki? I'm scared Daddy will find out if we do something to our sneakers. You know how Daddy is about our shoes," I said nervously.

"Go on, Trudi. We need to be quick!"

She said we needed the heavy scissors from our kitchen upstairs.

I ran up to get them.

Vicki and I stayed in the bedroom downstairs. We had a double bed, a five-drawer dresser, a vanity with a mirror, a bench, six small drawers, and a closet with two sliding doors. The walls and furniture were knotty pine wood. Outside our bedroom was a fully equipped kitchen with a washer and dryer, a family room with a couch, chairs, television, a built-in bar, a bathroom, and a large storage room with a cedar-lined closet. All the rooms were knotty pine wood.

I got the heavy scissors from the upstairs kitchen drawer and walked carefully down the stairs, holding them by their closed blades. Vicki hurried me into the bedroom and locked the bedroom door.

She started cutting the tops off the tennis shoes. "I'm making our new tennis shoes," Vicki said. I was fascinated.

After she cut up three shoes, she said, "Your turn. You do the last one."

I took the scissors, picked up the uncut shoe, and opened the scissors to cut. My hands were too small and weak to cut the fabric.

"Hurry up, Trudi. Somebody may come down and wonder why the door is locked."

"I'm trying, but I can't cut hard enough. These scissors are too big for my hands, and I'm not strong enough to cut them."

"Try again."

I tried but couldn't do it.

"Give them here," Vicki said with slight agitation.

She cut the fourth top off the sneaker with no difficulty.

"Now go hide these tops." She handed me four jagged sneaker tops.

I nodded and thought of the ideal hiding place—the hamper.

We didn't want our parents to know we'd cut up our sneakers. High-top tennis shoes were out of fashion, but Daddy had spent a lot of money on them, so hiding their remains from our parents was our only option. The hamper was an inspired idea. They'll never look there.

Wrong. Mommy found the sneaker tops two days later while doing the laundry. When Daddy got home, he called us upstairs. He was holding the four tennis shoe tops. Vicki and I looked at each other.

"You girls are on punishment for a month, and you will wear the cut-up sneakers to school the whole month," Daddy said.

We groaned. But secretly we thought we got off easy. Usually, we got spanked.

Denver Public Schools

I fainted under the East High School clock, the inside focal point of the school. Everyone had to pass the clock to go to their classrooms. When I came to, I was lying on a table in the nurse's office. I felt awful. My lower stomach was cramping, my head was burning, I felt the need to vomit, and I had intense spasms. The nurse told me that my father was on the way to pick me up.

"What's wrong with me?"

"Your father will be here shortly."

"You must have told him what's wrong with me since he's coming to get me."

"Lay back down."

WINNING THE BATTLE AGAINST MYSELF

"I feel awful." I put my head on the pillow and closed my eyes. About ten minutes later, Daddy shook me lightly.

"Wake up, Trudi Babe. Let's go home."

We rode in silence. I was sure I was dying, and Daddy didn't want to tell me. We stopped at a shopping center near our house. Daddy got out.

He returned with a large brown paper bag. We rode the rest of the way home in silence.

My legs felt like rubber as I got out of the car. Daddy walked quickly ahead of me.

He unlocked the door and headed to the telephone.

"Your mother is on the phone. Come talk to her." I was sure my life was over.

Mommy explained that my menstrual cycle had started and told me to use the products in the bag Daddy bought.

I went into the bathroom and saw the brown bag. I pulled my panties down. Blood was in them. I was ashamed. I couldn't look at my father for a month.

As life continued, my periods had disabling pain, so much so that I couldn't perform daily tasks. My hysterectomy at age 45 was a blessing.

Practicing for the debutante ball was a real pain. The ball was a party intended to present young women into society, a "debut," and you had to be invited to be a "deb."

Families created debutante cotillions so their children could meet other affluent black children. Denver's black community was so small that it made the idea of "society" even more ridiculous.

The ball was aimed at refinement and served as an opportunity to build relationships. Social groups and institutions such as black churches, Links, Jack & Jill, and, in Denver, the Owls Club and a couple of black sororities usually funded black balls and cotillions. These all-black balls served a different purpose from that of their white counterparts in that they were, in some ways, an effort on the part of wealthy blacks to show off the black community in a dignified manner.

Edumacation

The ball incorporated community service into our training. An emphasis was placed on education, networking, fundraising, and community outreach. Incentives such as scholarships and grants were given to participating "debs" with lofty career and educational goals.

The ordeal made me feel like an object. It was a ludicrous farce. Being a debutante did not sit well with me, especially since my best friend, Pamela, wasn't invited to be an Owl "deb." Pamela became a debutante with another organization. At least I had Angie and Diane K, my childhood church and school friends, to suffer through the Owl rehearsals and ball with me.

Frankly, I viewed the ball as an exercise in classism and exclusion at the time. This event kept wealth and opportunity isolated within the upper-class ranks, shutting out young black women from disadvantaged backgrounds who may have benefitted from participating.

Then came the pageantry. The pageantry included the clothes, hair, and money: frothy floor-length white gowns, long white gloves, upswept hairdos with tendrils framing the face, and an average of $3,500 in expenses. In addition, there were administrative fees to participate, ads bought for the program books, and families had to purchase a table at the ball. There were also specific dress requirements, which amounted to a hefty wardrobe budget considering the rarity of the items, such as crinolines for the skirts. These expenses were too costly for underprivileged families, and many didn't have the time to prepare for a ball properly.

As an adult, I thought dressing girls in virginal white gowns and presenting them as potential marriage material was archaic. I found it a demeaning throwback to when women had little control over their destinies. Plus, the racism of having separate black and white debutante balls intertwined with the elitism of a fake aristocracy and economic discrimination was unfathomable.

On the other hand, many families found it meaningful, including mine.

WINNING THE BATTLE AGAINST MYSELF

Daddy told me that the history of being a debutante showed the importance of the father in the family, since the father served as his daughter's escort. He said, "The ball also changed the negative stereotypes of black women after abolishing slavery. It combatted the stereotype of broken black families by having the fathers proudly present their daughters, which in turn disputed the damaging misconception of black women being non-virtuous."

Mommy got into the act as well. "Trudi, I know that the beauty and etiquette of the event bore you and that you resent the rehearsals. But that's a small part of the debutante ball. In the old days, these balls were held to find husbands for the girls. Where I grew up in the South, debutante balls were about education, giving back to the community, raising money, and forming a network."

I had no chance against those arguments.

I met Ronnie through Vicki's boyfriend, Carl, when I was fifteen. Carl was the star basketball player on a rival school team. He had come over to see Vicki and brought Ronnie with him. We met the boys on the sidewalk outside our house. Ronnie fell in love with me immediately. He said his heart fell hard on the cement, and no one, but he, heard the impact.

I liked Ronnie, too. Two years later, I asked him to be my escort for the debutante ball. He said no. Pow! I had never requested a boy to accompany me anywhere. And he said no.

It wasn't until years later that I discovered his real reason for declining my invitation. Ronnie didn't have money to rent or buy a tuxedo for the debutante ball. He was eighteen, so my parents wouldn't have let me go out with an older boy anyway.

Before Ronnie turned my invitation down, he and I had become good friends, and we talked and talked at hayrides, skating parties, and dances. We were always so consumed in our conversations that we never participated with others at social events. He became my best boy pal.

Edumacation

Forty-five years later, after we were finally married, Ronnie told me that Daddy had said, "Girls like that don't go out with guys like you." Thankfully, Ronnie didn't listen to him.

On the night of the 1968 ball, I stood in a receiving line and was introduced to the audience. I was announced and trotted around the stage, guided by Daddy, who presented me. Then we promenaded around the dance floor as I twirled with Daddy.

Next, my escort joined me. I had a kind, well-bred, tall, polished, nice-looking escort, Jerry. He was a year behind me in school. We had participated in student government enterprises and became friends. I asked him to be my Owl's Club escort, and he accepted whether it was in the name of chivalry or social custom. Jerry was patient and punctual. He never complained about the farce of a debutante ball or the inconvenience and expense of having to wear a tuxedo and buy me a wrist corsage. I had nothing but respect for him. He was a perfect guy. There were after-parties and dinners, but I had no interest in prolonging the evening's agony. I got home before my parents and Vicki.

I was elected President of the Delegate Assembly at East High School in my senior year, 1968. The Delegate Assembly was a representative student body governing board from each homeroom, making it more significant, diverse, and democratic than the Student Council. We focused on real issues affecting our lives and the lives of others. We were involved in anti-Vietnam War protests, civil rights issues, and women's equality. In 1968, I received the East High School Senior Girl Leadership Award.

Scarred by tragedy, 1968 was the year that changed America forever. The Vietnam War brought the unpopular War to TV screens and into homes. On the eve of the 1968 election, Richard Nixon, who would become president, committed treason by telling Anna Chennault—president of Chinese Refugee Relief from 1962 to 1970—to work with South Vietnam to delay the end of the War so that he could get elected. Dr. Martin Luther King, Jr. was assassinated on April 4, sparking riots across the country. On the night of the California primary, June 5, Robert F. Kennedy was assassinated. The Democratic National Convention in August opened with thousands of students, antiwar activists, and others meeting a violent police response.

There were also powerful moments amongst the tragedy. Ones that made the news, and ones that didn't. The October 16 Summer Olympics in Mexico City saw athletes John Carlos and Tommie Smith bow their heads and raise their fists during The Star-Spangled Banner; and on December 24, aboard Apollo 8, Jim Lovell, Bill Anders, and Frank Borman became the first humans to orbit the moon.

After Dr. King's assassination on April 4, 1968, I listened to college representatives pitch their wares in the auditorium. The head of Denver's Black Panthers, Lauren Watson, a family friend, came into the auditorium to get me and said he wanted to take me home if rioting broke out.

But Daddy had already asked Tom Bowens of the Denver Nuggets basketball team, who lived in the community, to drive me home and wait until I got inside safely.

It was during 1968 that I developed my ideological underpinnings of civil rights. My sensibilities heightened. Previously, nothing but music had moved me, as Dr. King's assassination did.

The civil rights movement was part of a broader freedom movement containing different strategies competing for black loyalty.

The parallel movements had figures like Malcolm X and Dr. King. It encompassed what Malcolm X called "the brothers in the streets."

Initially, I was more intrigued by Malcolm X than Dr. Martin Luther King, Jr. Malcolm advocated for separatism and armed defense. Dr. King aimed to achieve integration and hoped that nonviolence would allay white fears of black vengeance by showing that blacks would not respond to white provocations.

I did not believe Dr. King's focus was that the black movement was solely a choice between violence and nonviolence. I thought nonviolent followers could dismiss critics as violent using a pacifist religious approach. And, I deduced that the will to defend rights at all costs was owed more to Malcolm than to Dr. King.

Changing black consciousness was a paramount concern for Malcolm. Dr. King's "content of our character" phase was a rallying cry against race-conscious policy intended to remedy inequality.

Then I read Dr King's Letters from Birmingham City Jail. He wrote that if nonviolence "had not emerged, I am convinced that by now, the streets of the South would be flowing with floods of blood. And I am further convinced that if our white brothers are dismissed as 'rabble rousers' and 'outside agitators'—those of us working through the channels of nonviolent direct action ... millions of Negroes, out of frustration and despair, will seek solace and security in black ideologies, a development that will lead inevitably to a frightening racial nightmare." He added that a black man had "many pent-up resentments and latent frustrations" and "if his repressed emotions do not come out in these nonviolent ways they will come out in ominous expressions of violence. This is not a threat; it is a fact of history."

What Dr. King taught me, in essence, was that morally, you cannot defeat the enemy by becoming the enemy. The nonviolent approach is radical. You force your humanity on your enemy.

In Malcolm X's speech, The Ballot or the Bullet, he said that to attain equal rights for blacks, he "believe[d] in action on all fronts by whatever means necessary. If we don't do something real soon, I think you'll have to agree that we're going to be forced either to use the ballot or the bullet."

Around the same time, the MOVE Organization, a black group led by John Africa, lived in 307 and 309 Palleton Avenue houses in West Philadelphia. They fed stray dogs, cats, and rats. Sanitation was a real problem. In May 1977, these conditions caused a dispute between MOVE and the police, not MOVE and the neighborhood. The city turned off electricity, heat, and water, brought food for babies only, not adults, and erected a blockade. Mayor Rizzo said, "What they need is a good bath and soap and water in their mouths."

Over 600 police officers, heavily armed, surrounded the MOVE houses. "Kill anything that moves," Joseph O'Neill, Police Commissioner, instructed the officers. The police drilled down into the basement and poured 250 gallons of water into the homes. A shot was heard, dogs ran, then many shots were fired. Police poured more water in and then—according to the police—used smoke. Tear gas, according to the MOVE victims. Officers were caught on film beating and kicking Delbert Africa—and worse. O'Neill said Delbert Africa was "a savage." Children were hit with nightsticks. The city ordered the building taken down immediately to destroy the evidence of their crimes.

What was happening?

My thinking evolved, and my self-discovery emerged. The assassinations and MOVE confrontation were catalytic and transformative moments for me.

Dr. King became more militant regarding economic justice for blacks, and Malcolm X changed his views on race during his pilgrimage to Mecca. I now agreed with Dr. King that whites would feel justified in killing blacks without a multiracial, nonviolent approach on the part of blacks. I also trusted his view that one had to experience violence in order to be nonviolent.

In 1972, James Baldwin wrote "The Shot That Echoes Still," a painful and personal essay for Esquire magazine reflecting on the assassinations of Malcolm X in 1965 and Martin Luther King Jr. in 1968. Baldwin asserted that the two giants of the black power and civil rights movements, respectively, had begun "at what seemed to be very different points," but "by the time each met his death, there was practically no difference between them."

The world looked different to me after King's assassination. Would this change hearts and minds enough to live in the theoretical world I wanted to live in? Or would it be better to act out my rage and accomplish nothing?

Mama Briggs' words came back to me: use your head, not your fists.

Meanwhile, riots were breaking out all over the country, including Denver. In August 1968, my parents tried to tap down the incipient rage by establishing community watch groups and labeling the few Negro-owned businesses "Black-Owned."

I worked at a bank owned by a black man, Mr. Earl West, who hired me because he knew what kind of family I had. He understood what my parents were trying to do. We funded Black-Owned businesses, so Mr. West and the black community would have lost the bank if there were urban riots.

Assassinations, riots, property destruction, loss of life: what was the clash and dichotomy between what was going on in the streets and a black girl coming of age as a trained classical musician, as a child of privilege from a family that hated violence, as a girl who valued culture and classical art and language? Who was I, and who did I want to be? What did I have to work with to get where I wanted to be? Where did I fit? Where was I meant to serve? What skills, intuitive motivations, and reactions were within me? How did the culture in which I was raised tie into all of this?

I wasn't sure. I was confused.

Colorado State University: Part 1

In the Fall of 1967, I decided it was time to consider college. I made an appointment to meet with my high school counselor. My white female high school counselor told me I had a better chance of admittance to a two-year college than to a four-year university. Despite my grades, standardized test scores, and extracurricular activities, the counselor said that "my people did 'better' at two-year schools than four-year institutions."

"What do you mean, 'my people?'" I asked.

"It's just that minority students tend to be represented in higher numbers at two-year institutions," she said.

WINNING THE BATTLE AGAINST MYSELF

"How do you know that; why are you telling me this? Are you saying this because you are white and I'm not?" I pushed.

"Of course not. Race has nothing to do with it. How could you think that about me? It's simply that research shows that enrollments of minority students are far higher in community colleges than in many non-minority-serving four-year institutions," she said.

"The word 'minority' implies majority and two-year schools don't offer the range of majors as four-year schools, so what you said does have something to do with race," I argued.

Silence.

She'll never help me now. I should've kept my mouth shut, I thought.

I continued, "Well, I'll come back tomorrow during my lunch break to look at the research you're talking about. But I've always wanted to go to Colorado State University in Fort Collins, Colorado." I stood and walked out of her office. I wasn't upset or disappointed. I figured she didn't know what she was talking about.

She called in sick the next day. I didn't follow up.

I was admitted to the four-year institution Colorado State University (CSU) in Fort Collins, Colorado. Fort Collins was a beautiful city nestled in the foothills of the Rocky Mountains. I applied for a music scholarship but received a reply stating that awards were not given for the string bass. I didn't understand. I wrote an essay about why the bass violin was the backbone of the orchestra. The spine was always the string section, and the double bass was always the backbone of the string section. Therefore, the string bass was the backbone of the orchestra. The music department was impressed with my plea. I earned academic and music scholarships to CSU, but I still needed the U.S. Savings Bonds Mommy and Daddy kept in a shoe box under their bed.

I had excellent grades throughout high school and college except for the "D" I got in Biology of Plants since I preferred

Edumacation

learning to play Bid Whist in CSU's Ramskeller instead of going to class at 2:00 pm. every day.

I majored in psychology and minored in music. At that time, I had narrowed my interests to law or medicine. I approached my major as an exercise to understand people's nature and read motives and intents because I knew I would need that knowledge, whether I chose law or medicine for a career. It's also why I took Latin in high school. That was a trip in and of itself. East High School had no Latin course, so they found someone and hired him to teach me Latin. I was his only student.

Professor Robert Titley, head of the Psychology Department at CSU, was my teacher and counselor. Dr. T taught me to live and learn with humor.

The string bass became my alter ego, shadow, and reflection at CSU. My best friend, Pamela and I carried it in the snow from the music department past Moby Gym to the off-campus Cambridge House. I had the most fantastic orchestra teacher in the world, Maestro Wilfred Schwartz. He saw my potential when I auditioned for him in high school. A young black woman playing a blond bass violin was an oddity. Mr. Schwartz invested time and energy in me. He encouraged me to pursue a career in music and complimented my existing appreciation for classical music.

His teaching will continue through the influence of those students who were blessed enough to have studied with him. Because of him, I was the first student invited to play with the Fort Collins Symphony Orchestra. There were no other black musicians in the orchestra. I made myself belong. I refused to be alienated. I wouldn't let prejudice or racism deter me from my music. After all, my musical heritage informed my musical abilities. I was sure that my grandfather, father, aunt, and cousin experienced bigotry and hatred because of their race; but even so, Big Daddy became a renowned jazz band leader and violinist; Daddy played the violin each Sunday at church for sixty years; Auntie Marian taught piano in two Denver Public

WINNING THE BATTLE AGAINST MYSELF

Schools and gave private lessons for more than fifty years; and cousin Georgie was the rehearsal pianist for the Stuttgart Ballet for forty-one years.

At one of my concerts, I glanced at the audience while tuning my bass and situating the music on my stand. "What the heck?" I couldn't believe my eyes. The football and basketball teams occupied the entire front row with shaved heads and sideburns! I laughed out loud. The heads in the cello section turned toward me. I put my hand over my mouth. The front row of shaved heads with sideburns stood and nodded at me. They were there for me. What was going on? Who orchestrated (excuse the pun) this? These guys didn't like classical music. I bet they had never been to a symphony concert. Whose idea was this? Which of them knew I had a concert today? Why were they all supporting me?

This was an act of love. I realized that although I was still overwhelmed. I never found out who instigated that unforgettable surprise.

Playing in the Fort Collins Symphony Orchestra took me off-campus for rehearsals and concerts. Black students faced off-campus housing discrimination in the 1970s. Although the University did not try to control students' lives by deciding what was adequate housing, black off-campus students had to live well beyond the campus neighborhood because closer housing was cost-prohibitive This resulted in commutes, which often made it impossible to work evenings.

Our knowledge of off-campus houses that would not rent to black students added to the frustration.

While practicing for concerts, I always had to navigate who I was as a black person. Feeling the direct blow of off-campus discrimination, I began pressuring the CSU administration to improve off-campus housing conditions.

I grew tired of feeling like an outsider unless I was playing my music. While off-campus, playing my rapturous bass was the only time I felt like I was seen as a person in my own right, not merely by the color of my skin. Music was a great equalizer for me.

Colorado State University: Part II

Pamela—my friend since seventh grade—and I were lucky to be college roommates. The day we met, after a day of sitting near each other in some classes, I turned and asked her name.

She said, "Pamela."

I said, "Oh," and turned back around.

No more words were spoken between us that day.

Pam had an older brother, an older sister, and twin younger sisters. The twins were a hoot. Not only were the fraternal twins gorgeous, but they also had a wickedly dry sense of humor. They would do strange things like staring at me non-stop without saying a word.

Pam had lovely long, thick jet-black hair. In those days, some black girls pressed, that is, straightened their hair with a hot comb. Whenever I did Pam's hair, I would sweat so much that my hair immediately reverted, causing my hair to curl up again.

I wanted to wear my hair afro style, but the curls wouldn't stay in very long. I teased and teased my hair until a lot of it fell out.

When I went home for Thanksgiving, my mother took one look at my hair and forced me to go to Olin Mills, an expensive photography studio, for a portrait showing my near baldness. She said she wanted me to look at that photo, so I'd never forget how I ruined my hair.

A few months later, Vicki and I bought afro wigs, went to Jafay, another costly photography studio, and gave Mommy and Daddy a 16" x 16" photograph in a gold gilded frame of us in Afro wigs for Christmas. The photo still hangs in their living room.

My mother bought Pam and me matching bedspreads to coordinate the look of our dorm room.

The day we moved into the dorm, a white girl came to our room and asked, in a demeaning, imitating dialect, if she could touch me. Startled, we wondered why. She replied that she had always heard that people would get burned if they felt a Negro.

Young and reckless, I physically threw her out of our room. Early on, I realized that white expectations and fears took up too much time. I thought she was emotionally ignorant. Looking into the white girl's eyes, I saw an empty pool of altruism concerning black humanity.

Like my stupidity in letting Vicki bind my leg before cutting it for bacon, I took another bodily chance by allowing Pamela to pierce my ears with a needle and straw from a broom.

She was confident in her ear-piercing prowess. We numbed my ears with ice cubes; Pam wiped the needle with alcohol, then burned the tip of a sewing needle to disinfect it. There was no marking the spot on my ear to insert the needle.

Aside from pain and terror, the left ear piercing went well. Pam broke a piece of straw off a broom, burned it, and wiped it with alcohol. She put it in my ear, rotated the straw, and drenched my ear in alcohol. Then she saturated my left ear with camphor oil. How impressive!

The right ear was a nightmare. The needle wouldn't go through cartilage. Pamela pushed the needle through as straight and swiftly as possible, but the longer she pushed, the more my ear would hurt. We took a break.

Pam put more alcohol on a cotton ball and squeezed it on my left ear. My right ear was throbbing.

"Let's go ahead and get this over," I pleaded.

"I agree."

Pam pushed the needle harder, and it broke through the cartilage. She followed the same routine she administered to my left ear, but was extra gentle on the red, puffy right ear.

To this day, I have trouble putting earrings in that ear because the line isn't straight; it curves awkwardly.

Ronnie would come up to CSU with Carl for parties. I had no idea he was coming up to see me, as he never showed any romantic interest in me. At one party, he asked me for a cup of punch. I wasn't hosting the party, and it wasn't my apartment. I interpreted his request as a rude order, a demand ... and walked away from him, still smarting from his refusal to escort me to the debutante ball two years prior. I was hurt because Ronnie and I had been such good friends, and now I viewed him as a foe. It was hard having a crush on an enemy. I didn't know and what he didn't tell me was that he was shipping out the following day to Travis Air Force Base in San Francisco on his way to Vietnam.

Colorado State University: Part III

In 1984, I received CSU's first William E. Morgan Alumni Achievement Award, the highest honor given and reserved for alums who have excelled at the national or international level.

Ironically, the award was named for the same president I had vigorously opposed in 1969, William E. Morgan.

Figure 16. -Trudi holding microphone while CSU's President William E. Morgan explains CSU's position. Pamela, second from left.

Because of the late 1960s campus unrest focusing on student rights, civil rights, and Vietnam War opposition becoming a major institutional issue, Morgan retired as president effective June 1969.

In the Collegian, the CSU newspaper, I got a column where my byline was "To The White Pigs Governing or Attending This University." I was radicalized: music career out; law career in.

WINNING THE BATTLE AGAINST MYSELF

In 1969, I was elected to the student governing body, the Associated Students of Colorado State University, on The New Priorities Party platform. Don, the organizer of the group, was the catalyst behind this vision and became president. Rich Witkin, Norm Ruggles, Karen Layton, and Brad Pierce were my other student government colleagues. I think of them often.

In February 1970, at the DPS school bus depot on Seventh Avenue near Federal Boulevard in Denver, a series of explosions traveled down a line of school buses parked so close together that the flames leaped from one to another, destroying nearly one-third of the fleet. The act appeared to be a reaction to a lawsuit filed by eight Denver families in 1969 (my family did not join the case), which argued that DPS schools—particularly in northeast Denver, where I grew up—were segregated and provided unequal education. The question was used to integrate schools into neighborhoods that were decidedly not. The District Court agreed with the plaintiffs.

I don't know exactly why my parents didn't join the lawsuit. Perhaps it was because Daddy worked for the DPS. Or, maybe it was because they didn't support busing since they thought the pool of white students would decline to a point where busing achieved nothing—no integration. It took twenty-six years to end forced busing in Denver.

In October 1970, eight months after the February 1970 series of explosions of school buses in Denver, destroying nearly one-third of the fleet, I became Colorado State University's first black Homecoming Queen. Those acts were polar opposites in terms of civil rights progress.

The Black Student Alliance, the entity founded by Meredith Springs, Paul Chambers, and me, gave black students a kind of timid pride, making us unified and not just a handful of socially isolated cliques. The first director of the Black/African American Cultural Center was Vivian Kerr. Vivian had also been an undergraduate student involved in our protests.

Edumacation

Sadly, the Black Student Alliance failed to support me for Homecoming Queen and ran a friend against me, arguing, "I already had too much." I felt betrayed by my people.

Coincidentally, the 1970 Homecoming Dance boasted CSU's first entertainer of color, Puerto Rican genius Jose Feliciano. That evening, Mr. Feliciano invited me to the stage to honor my victory as Homecoming Queen. I went on stage, and Mr. Feliciano held our joined hands in the air. The crowd went crazy.

In my elation, I raised a fist in the air. Raising my fist in the air was about joy for the hope of equality. Some misinterpreted my action as threatening toward white students. My joy spawned hues and cries for months through aggressive letter-writing campaigns in the Collegian. I fought back, word-for-word. Black celebration and exuberance have constantly been scrutinized and negatively critiqued by whites, whether spiking a football, dunking a basketball, or raising a fist in the air.

Were these the same students dismayed by and antagonistic toward my joyous fist gesture earlier that day? I had no idea, but I was smart enough to smile, wave, and get off the stage as soon as possible.

The following morning, while walking to the Student Union, Vicki pushed me into the gutter to avoid a car that lurched toward me at increasing speed. Later that evening, someone threw a brick through my apartment window.

Were these my fans from yesterday's Homecoming events? Odds were, they weren't. There were 17,000 students, less than 50 of whom were black, and I won by 400 votes.

My election was particularly notable, as it took nearly twenty years for CSU to have its second black Homecoming Queen, and no controversy surrounded her election, unlike the vitriol of my election in 1970.

The students who tried to minimize or destroy my accomplishments failed to see reality: I was elected as a student government leader for the entire student body, not a monolithic portion. I was elected Homecoming Queen by the student body, not by a racial or ethnic part of the student body. Prejudice and jealousy didn't belong to me—they belonged to those who hated me.

In the mid-2000s, I became a Monfort Scholar-in-Residence at CSU, a program designed to bring accomplished individuals in business, government, and the arts to campus from around the world to provide leadership enrichment opportunities for high-achieving students. I keynoted two Black History Month celebrations and was profiled as the 1970s alumna in CSU's The Magazine (Spring 2018). This profile was particularly remarkable, encompassing ten years of CSU alums: 1970-1979.

Colorado State University: Part IV

Pamela and I had great parties. Our two-bedroom apartment had a kitchen, a bathroom, and a sizable living room. Furniture was sparse: a couch, bookcase, two tables with lamps, and a desk, making it easy to accommodate twenty-five people in the living room.

We lived on the fourth floor of a five-story building. There was no elevator; the walls were painted pea green and the doors bright orange. The one window in the apartment was in my room and faced a brick wall.

"I'll call Vicki and ask her to make potato salad when she comes up," I said.

Pamela nodded assent. Vicki moved back home after attending college. She experienced the trauma of a dorm neighbor committing suicide.

Vicki sent me packages every week. Cookies, clothes, and records. Records were vinyl 45s with picture sleeves. Each 45 was printed in a different color.

Pam was an excellent cook and enjoyed cooking. She grilled three chickens and roasted a beef roast that we got free from the grocery store where Nancy, who dropped out of school, was a checker. Pam and I couldn't afford meat but paid for fresh vegetables and canned goods.

Edumacation

With no word from Ronnie, and not knowing he was in Vietnam, I fell for someone I knew couldn't be my forever love.

Sitting on a bench at an off-campus party, I suddenly felt a hot breath and a kiss on my neck. It was my not-forever-love. I kissed him. "Shall we dance?" I asked. I thought of the musical The King and I. In the musical, the King of Siam, Thailand, and Anna, the live-in governess to the King of Siam's children, fell in love while dancing. My not-forever-love and I danced to The Sweeter He Is by the Soul Children. The earth stopped rotating.

My parents took Vicki and me to open-air performances of Broadway musicals sponsored by Denver Post Operas in Cheesman Park. Situated on eighty acres, the Cheesman Park neighborhood was urban, with large mansions for some of the city's wealthiest people. My parents, Vicki, and I had picnics under shade trees before the program started and a ceiling of twinkling stars during the presentation. The King and I was one of the plays we saw. We also saw South Pacific, Oklahoma, and Show Boat.

The orchestra in the pit below the stage captivated me: the bowed strings vibrated, sending waves of harmonics; the percussion clashed and clanged; the woodwinds sang as silver keys depressed and released, allowing air to pass through differing lengths of the instrument; the brass kissed with lips against fitted vibrating mouthpieces; the keyboard plucked or struck stretched and tuned strings.

I met my not-forever-love on my first day at CSU in Ellis Hall. Pam and I were moving into the dorm and took a break for outside air. My not-forever-love and his roommate were already outside checking out the girls moving in. He came over to me and kissed me on the lips. He had a gold tooth. I had never seen anyone with a gold tooth. I slapped my not-forever-love and ran inside the dorm. Right then and there, I decided to hate him forever.

I'd eventually find that was a lie I told myself, but not before dating another man, Archie.

WINNING THE BATTLE AGAINST MYSELF

The first time I saw Archie, he walked across campus in a pink and black dashiki. Dashikis were shirts that originated in West Africa as a functional work tunic for men. They became popular during the Civil Rights and Black Panther movements in the late 1960s and early 1970s. That clothing was not intended to be fanciful. Dashikis showed pride in our African culture.

Archie was tall and handsome and sported a slightly crooked Afro. The Afro was a symbol of pride and resistance among the black community. Archie's Afro hair was cut into a full, bushy shape all over his head. He was one of CSU's star basketball players. The Collegian dubbed him "The Gentle Giant."

I had never known a kinder, more compassionate person. And he loved me. We were together whenever free time allowed. Archie was the first man I took to Denver to meet my parents. They loved him. Over the years, Archie became a trusted friend of our family.

During my second year, Archie went to Belgium to play basketball.

Meanwhile, Carl, Vicki's boyfriend, and his friend, Ricky, came to CSU for two or three parties. Ricky and I talked and danced at each of those parties. Ricky and Carl were the star basketball players on the Wyoming team.

Ricky and I wrote letters to each other for a year or more. Yes, letters with a pen and paper. I had cute stationery Georgie sent. Ricky's words lifted me through difficult days and snowy nights. Although Ricky and I could have become more than platonic friends, I could only think of Ronnie when I saw Carl. Have you heard from Ronnie? How is he? Where is he? What is he doing? Does he have a girlfriend? When is he coming back to Colorado? Carl should have been ashamed of himself for bringing Ricky to me, a man I could have loved when he was supposed to be Ronnie's best friend. I never trusted Carl.

In the meantime, my hate for my not-forever-love morphed into a love for him. Hate and love are dual emotions. I remember the moment my feelings changed from hate to love.

Edumacation

His roommate was killed in a tragic car accident. Both of us traveled to Memphis for the funeral. I spoke as the CSU representative. During those days away from school, mourning our mutual friend, we shared experiences and spent much time together. Grief provided the turning point in our relationship. My not-forever-love told me I "was used to rugs, and he would give me carpets." Now, that was true love.

We spent a summer together when I attended summer school in Fort Collins. I rented a house on South Loomis Street, within walking distance of campus. My not-forever-love came over during evenings and, sometimes, afternoons. We talked, laughed, ate, and made love. His firm, cleat-scarred hands caressed my breasts, and I ran my fingers through the hair on his chest. He had a beautiful body, so manly, so sexy. He'd run his tongue over my teeth when we kissed. I wanted to taste every part of him. When his penis penetrated my body, the hypersensitive nerve endings in my vagina were on fire. He moved slowly and in a relaxed way, elevating my level of arousal.

One evening my not-forever-love took me to dinner at a hotel in Loveland, Colorado. Loveland was 30 minutes from the Fort Collins campus. After dinner, I excused myself to go to the restroom. When I came out, my not-forever-love was waiting for me in the hallway. My heart melted when I looked into his eyes. He grabbed me by the waist, pulling me into him. My feet and common sense left the ground, orbiting another galaxy. His lips kissed my cheek; I turned my head to meet his mouth. I wanted every part of him. He sensed my need, "Let's go."

"Okay," I murmured. We drove to my house and made love until the following day.

As happens in life, my not-forever-love and I went our separate ways, on separate coasts, with different lifestyles. We traveled between Los Angeles and Washington, DC, throughout my law school years. But I knew from its beginning that mine was the love of a young woman who was keenly aware that her passion was too intense, too consuming to last.

WINNING THE BATTLE AGAINST MYSELF

Those college years were when I experienced the most passionate love I had known and would ever know. Our relationship was playful, ardent, and intense. Somehow, I managed to keep my wits about me so as not to circumvent my future aspirations with marriage or pregnancy. I wouldn't have been able to handle the exhaustion from splitting my attention between school and getting prepared for a baby. I couldn't imagine sacrificing those "fun" aspects of my 20s to make room for diaper changes and late-night feedings.

Colorado State University: Part V

I had never heard of the Law School Admittance Test (LSAT). My student government colleague, Rich Witkin, vice president of the CSU student body, planned to attend law school at the University of Michigan. As student government leaders, we became good friends and often discussed the law.

Rich left his bright blue stick-shift Camaro with me during one of the holidays. It was parked outside my dorm in the sloped circular driveway. And wouldn't you know it? I had never seen street cleaning trucks on campus before, but they came and left a notice on Rich's windshield to move the vehicle or have it towed.

The car had different pedals and a gear shift. I got in the car, put my right foot on the brake, pushed the left pedal down (called the clutch) to the floorboard, and turned on the ignition to start the car. I put my right foot on the accelerator and lifted my left foot off the clutch quickly. The car jumped and went dead. I thought that was good and bad. Good because the car didn't move; bad because the car didn't move. I surmised that I was clueless. I pressed the accelerator too lightly because my flip-flops slipped off the right pedal.

With the next attempt, I put on my flats from my tote bag and placed my right foot on the brake. I slowly put less pressure on the left pedal and gently pressed the accelerator. The car moved without jerking. My confidence resurfaced. I put more

Edumacation

pressure on the accelerator and heard the motor straining. I knew that meant I needed to shift the car into second gear.

Based on what Rich said, I took my right foot off the accelerator and placed my left foot on the clutch. I tried to move the gear shifter into second gear, but it seemed stuck. I tried again, and it worked. I let up on the clutch and pushed down harder on the accelerator. I was driving a stick-shift car!

When Rich returned, he told me he was driving to Denver to take the LSAT on Saturday. He said I should come with him and take the exam. I asked how much it cost, and he said he would pay the $10.00 fee.

Early Saturday morning Rich and I drove to Denver for the test. Rich made me aware of a preparatory course by Kaplan, but I didn't have time to take the class. When Rich and I walked in, the auditorium was full of hopeful exam-takers. These folks were serious, and I overheard many comparing preparatory courses and their costs. I was there, so I figured I might as well take a shot at it.

The LSAT tested whether you had the required skills and competence to cope with the challenging law school curriculum. You didn't need prior legal knowledge to pass the test, but you did need excellent reading comprehension and analytical and logical reasoning skills. I did alright on the test, crafted a personal statement, asked Dr. Titley for a recommendation letter, and sent resumes and the required photographs to the law schools of my choice.

Requiring photos disturbed me. Why did law schools need pictures of applicants? Were their motives good or bad, and what could good or bad mean? Was this about affirmative action? Race? Gender? I wanted to be accepted at a school in Washington, DC, so these meaningful questions disappeared. Rich and I got into our law school choices: Michigan, his home state, and me to Washington, DC, because of my interest in politics and law.

A month before leaving Denver for law school, I was a runner-up in the Miss Black Colorado Pageant. Entrants had sponsors, individuals, or groups that paid that candidate's expenses and spent money on advertising. My sponsor was The Denver Drum, the local black newspaper Syl Morgan-Smith published. Syl was a longtime family friend, a glamorous, wonderful lady, and a continual blessing to many. She was instrumental in telling me and showing me the importance of preparing for those coming after us. I had never been in a contest before, but I entered the competition because the prize was $750.00.

"You shouldn't play that piece in the talent part of the competition, Trudi Michelle. It won't be as relatable to the audience as a more well-known piece. It's too high brow. I think the judges will mark you down for playing a classical piece," Daddy said.

The piano piece I wanted to play was Nocturne in C sharp minor by Frédéric François Chopin.

"I don't have time to memorize another piece, Daddy."

"Let her play what she's comfortable with, George," Mommy said.

"She's making a mistake. She has time to memorize another piece if she gets started now."

"I don't have enough time," I stated vehemently.

"Stop making excuses. You could do it if you wanted to. You're just being lazy." Daddy's words stung.

My eyes teared.

"George, leave her alone."

"This is a mistake," Daddy said and stormed out of the room.

I played the Chopin piece and received polite applause. At that moment, I knew my father was correct about my musical selection.

As I write, I remember the young and the old Daddy. I don't want to lose the memories of time: What, possibly, did he do for two hours in the bathroom each day? Why did he prefer his shirts laundered with little starch and returned in boxes, not hangers? Why did he get his haircut in the same Five Points barber shop throughout his life? Why would he sneak in the side door with packages of clothes he hid in the basement? Why would he fry shrimp one at a time? Why were his kisses so wet? Why did he insist I wear a bra when I was twenty-two? Why did he trim the lawn closest to the house with scissors? Why did he prefer Winchell's Donuts to Krispy Kreme donuts? Why did he always smell so good? Why? Why? Why?

Going back to the Miss Black Colorado Pageant, walking across the stage in a swimsuit, I was mortified, taking extra-long strides toward the curtain leading off-stage. I did, however, win the swimsuit competition.

"The winners will entertain a gathering at the moderator's home tomorrow afternoon," the announcer said.

As a finalist, I had to show up.

The next afternoon our job was to model clothes, including swimsuits, around the pool and serve drinks to the guests. Oh, no. A swimsuit in public again. The money isn't worth it.

I was up next. As I walked by the pool, a tree branch lifted the wig from my head and dropped it into the swimming pool — the audience gasped. I felt naked. I had to rebound from this—immediately. I calmly bent down and retrieved the wig, wrung it out, placed it back on my stocking-capped head, and strutted off as if nothing had happened.

"Vicki, Vicki," I yelled as I ran into the dressing room.

"I'm over here. What happened?"

I was babbling; I couldn't find the words. "Slow down, Trudi. I can't understand you."

"My wig fell into the swimming pool."

"What? It's out there floating around the pool?" Vicki asked with a slight giggle.

"No, this is it," I said, pointing to my head as water dripped down my face.

"Are you ok?"

I looked at her.

"Who got it out of the pool?"

"I did. I fished it out," I said.

Another giggle escaped her.

WINNING THE BATTLE AGAINST MYSELF

"You know you have to go back out there."

"I know."

"Just act like nothing happened. And pin it on this time!"

"I will. Thanks."

When I walked out again, modeling another designer outfit, the announcer said, "That is why she's a winner—cool and confident."

Edumacation

Figure 17. -Trudi - Winner of 1972 Miss Black Colorado Swimsuit Competition.

Chapter 8

The Lost World

"You can't lose what you don't own."
-Toni Morrison

The National Law Center at George Washington University

I got into The National Law Center at George Washington University (GW) on a full academic scholarship and flew to Washington, DC, early for an orientation session. My parents hired a professional service to drive out my yellow Maverick. I had gotten the Maverick during my second year of college since the Valiant was getting too old.

A friend of my mother's had a family she was close to who offered to let me stay with them until the dorm opened.

The Joneses had an apartment over their garage. The room was an inverted triangle shape with two large windows facing the street. The chintz drapes matched the bedspread, wallpaper, and chair. The fabric and wallpaper were full of botanical, blossoming trees and luminous flowers. I now recall that the Palace of Versailles had chintz wallcoverings, settees, screens, and chairs just outside Paris. Chintz there was exquisite.

The Lost World

The Joneses were morticians. They were terrific people, but they discussed their work over dinner. One evening, they talked about a horrific accident on the Beltway, saying, "We got her in today, and we have a lot of work to do."

Morticians. How did I get into this situation? It was free. They had a beautiful home, provided three meals a day, and drove me to the law school so I'd know how to get there.

Bless them. I had never lived outside of Colorado. Washington, DC, was a different city in numerous ways. I had never noticed or appreciated the amount of land in Colorado. Buildings, homes, and establishments, including McDonald's, sprawled.

Everything was crammed together in the District and went up, not out. People were everywhere, leaving little room on sidewalks. Everyone rushed, even to stoplights. They talked rapidly and seldom smiled. At home, black people acknowledged each other on the streets. In DC, black people didn't seem to notice other black people. My GW class had few women and fewer blacks.

My undergraduate school, CSU, was in the lower hills of the majestic Rocky Mountains. GW sat in a cement jungle four blocks from the White House. Colorado had dramatic wilderness and diverse wildlife. Bighorn Sheep ruled the Rockies. Foggy Bottom in downtown Washington, the Northwest quadrant where GW was located, lacked grass, trees, and housed rats.

One day, when my friend Lee and I were sitting in my dorm room, a giant insect crawled out of a crack in the wall and made its home on my bookcase. I screamed at the top of my lungs.

"What is that?" I asked. Jeanette and Peter ran into the room. They saw the critter and laughed.

Lee said, "It's a baby roach." I shuddered to think what an adult roach looked like. The nasty thing was gigantic.

"We have roaches the size of rats in New York. Once, I saw a roach eat a rat," Jeanette said.

"Stop it, guys," I said.

WINNING THE BATTLE AGAINST MYSELF

Peter said, "Let's get something to eat before your roommate returns."

Figure 18. -Lee and Trudi at law school graduation (1975).

I had a white roommate, Liz. Her hair would continually clog the shower drain. The straggly hair would wrap itself around my toes — ick! I had to get Liz out of the room because she had sex with her boyfriend when I was trying to study or sleep. Asses going up and down were distracting. More upsetting was that Liz defiled the bedspread Mommy sent. She and her boyfriend stained the spread with body excretions during their sexual adventures.

I went to the resident hall leader and told her what happened and that, as a law student studying at night, I didn't need to be looking at naked behinds. They kicked Liz out of the dorm after paying the bedspread's cleaning bill. I had a solo room after that.

The Lost World

Driving in and around Washington was not child's play. Washington, DC, had many "circles": Dupont Circle, Logan Circle, Thomas Circle, Sheridan Circle, Sherman Circle, Grant Circle, Ward Circle, and Anna J. Cooper Circle. I would have liked to meet the Frenchman, L'Enfant, who laid out the city and give him a piece of my mind. What was wrong with that man? These circles were traffic nightmares.

Thomas Circle, Scott Circle, Logan Circle, and Dupont Circle were all relatively close, so I followed the wrong circle repeatedly. The street near American University where I later taught, Ward Circle, begged the question, "Why are we turning right to go left?" I never got an answer.

As bad as the circles were, the Beltway was from Hell. The Capital Beltway was a 64-mile Interstate Highway surrounding Washington, DC, and its inner suburbs in adjacent Maryland and Virginia. If you don't get off, it takes an hour and 20 minutes to go around. Guess how I know that? You got it right! Yes, I rounded it three times on the same day and needed to remember where I was headed.

The police officer who stopped me after observing my out-of-state license plates and three Beltway tours said, "There are two directions of travel, clockwise and counterclockwise, the Inner Loop and the Outer Loop."

"I beg your pardon?"

"Traffic congestion, traffic jams, and a high volume of vehicles on both the inner and outer loops of the Beltway are a problem. Estimates say that about 225,000 cars use the Beltway each workday, with volumes increasing even more during holidays and summer months."

"Have I done something, officer?"

"No, but the Beltway is a dangerous highway. There are multiple lanes, rushed commuters, congested traffic, and sometimes speeding or reckless drivers. You need to avoid it."

"Thanks, officer, but how do I return to Washington?"

"Follow me."

WINNING THE BATTLE AGAINST MYSELF

He got back in his car and led me to the District line.

Over the years, I got comfortable with the Beltway and drove it daily. When the Beltway wasn't bottle-necked, there was nothing like it.

I met Roslyn a few days after classes started. She was from New York City and drove an orange 2-door coupe Opel GT. It had pop-up and down headlights. Cool. I liked Roslyn despite her overly competitive nature. Lee saw through her right away and warned me not to trust her.

She made derogatory remarks about Lee's hometown, Natchez, Mississippi, showing her ignorance. Roslyn spoke about the historical remnants and present manifestations of authoritarian racism.

"Yesum, Massa," Roslyn would say to Lee while shuffling her feet, bulging, and popping her eyes. Lee was right about her from the beginning.

It took a while to understand that she used me to draw light-complexioned black men to her. Roslyn could get my leftovers if I weren't interested in the guy.

Roslyn took me to Howard University, a Historically Black University, on a sunny afternoon. After CSU, I should have expected any school setting to be disappointing. Howard fit the bill. I had a similar reaction when I saw Motown in Detroit. Motown was a tiny house. Those two institutions taught me a lot about life. Greatness can come in small packages.

When we got to Howard's campus, Roslyn whispered, "We only speak to men in law or medical school." The statement itself was curious, but the whispering was downright weird.

"Why are you whispering and acting strange?"

"Come on," she said. We walked into one of the students' gathering places, and a guy was sitting in the middle of the room in a chair resembling a throne. The throne had a rich purple velvet seat above an ornate, carved skirt. The legs were gold lion paws, and the arms were griffins. A griffin was a legendary creature with the body, tail, and back legs of a lion, the head and wings of an eagle. In Dante Alighieri's Divine Comedy, after Dante and Virgil's journey through Hell and Purgatory had concluded, Dante met a chariot dragged by a griffin in Earthly Paradise. Immediately afterward, Dante was reunited with Beatrice. Dante and Beatrice then started their journey through Paradise.

"Who's that?" I asked, laughing out loud.

"Shhh... His name is Adam," Roslyn whispered.

"You mean like the first earthly man?" I asked, while laughing again.

Adam was light-complexioned, uncommonly handsome, and had "good hair"- the name coined by past generational blacks (presumably others).

"Good hair" was not kinky, curly, or nappy hair. It was a hair closer to the texture of people from Europe, Asia, or the Middle East, but not sub-Saharan Africa. Black hair had been the centerpiece for how blacks viewed themselves (possibly a gross overstatement now, but not when I was growing up).

Anyway, the first earthly man had a loose hair texture and had, undoubtedly, gotten more privilege in society than those who did not possess these features.

Adam looked me up and down and gestured to a seat before his throne for me to rest my peasant's bones.

I declined and asked, "What is this? What's going on?"

The first earthly man spoke, "What kind of car does your father drive?"

I said, "He drives your mother's car, you pompous ass!" Talking about someone's mother was called "playing the dozens." I was trash-talking.

I turned to Roslyn and said, "Just take me back to the dorm."

Roslyn appeared to believe that light skin was more attractive than dark skin. She was dark-skinned and pretty. Until then, I hadn't been directly exposed to color discrimination among black people. To me, discrimination was discrimination, and all of it wasn't good.

WINNING THE BATTLE AGAINST MYSELF

Deep down, Roslyn abhorred her skin color. She was a victim of colorism and shadism and the social implications attached to skin color. Colorism was prejudice based on skin tone, preferring lighter skin tones. Shadism was based on a skin color hierarchy, giving lighter skin tones privileges. Researchers found men were subconsciously attracted to fairer skin due to its association with purity, innocence, modesty, and goodness. At the same time, women felt that darker complexions were associated with sex, masculinity, and danger.

I thought mixed-race births only complicated this issue. These children of mixed birth, born after 1967, were part of the Loving Generation. The parents of these mixed-race kids were allowed to marry because of the Supreme Court ruling in Loving v. Virginia, the 1967 case striking down laws banning interracial marriage.

I read a Pew Research article informing that multiracial adults who were seen by others as white were far less likely to say they had faced discrimination across several measures than those who were black, Hispanic, or multiracial. In addition, biracial adults who were white and black had a more positive view of the impact of their racial background than did single-race blacks.

To me, another gross generalization came down to one factor: light skin remained ideal because it was preferred by the dominant group: white people.

I'd be remiss if I failed to mention a study published in the American Sociological Review that found that white people struggled to holistically identify people of color as individuals with unique attributes, including a limited capacity to perceive a variation in black skin shades. (Hill, Mark E. 2002. "Race of Interviewer and Perception of Skin Color: Evidence from the Multi-City Study of Urban Inequality." American Sociological Review 67(1):99–108).

I moved out of the dormitory during my second law school year. First-year law students, generally speaking, lived in the dormitory. I found an apartment in a lovely building at 2112 New Hampshire Avenue.

The Lost World

It was an Efficiency, one large room with a kitchenette and bathroom. Mommy and Daddy sent me a credit card to help furnish my apartment. I knew about an inexpensive furniture store on 7th and D streets, near Pennsylvania Avenue, called The Hub. I bought a green and gold pull-out sofa bed, two end tables, two table lamps, one-floor lamp, a bed frame and mattress, and a rug. They delivered. "Woodies," Woodward & Lothrop department store on 10th, 11th, F, and G Streets was ten stories tall and moderately priced. Parking was difficult in downtown Washington, and the parking meter folks wrote tickets before the meters expired.

Mayor Marion Barry instituted quotas for meter readers, so writing tickets became a competitive sport. I finally got a parking space three blocks from Woodies. Not thinking about hauling items to my three blocks away car, I bought two sheet sets, a bedspread, a blanket, pillows, a bathroom set, and kitchen towels and utensils. I convinced an employee to watch my packages while I got to my car. I double-parked and ran into Woodies to get my packages. Within the 3 minutes it took to retrieve my goods, I got a $75 ticket.

In addition to meeting Lee in law school, I met another lifelong friend, Marita. Marita and I attended different law schools. We met through my law school friend Jeanette, who attended undergraduate school with Marita in New York.

Figure 19. -Marita and Trudi, Marita's law school graduation, 1975.

WINNING THE BATTLE AGAINST MYSELF

We lived across the hall in my New Hampshire Avenue, NW apartment building, a block from a Howard University dormitory. A park separated the apartment building from the dormitory. It was a dangerous park. People were frequently assaulted there. Unfortunately, the park was the most direct way to get to the dormitory, so students took chances. I avoided the street facing the park as much as possible, but that was often the only place to find a parking space.

"C'mon bitch, or I'll slice you right here," a rich, masculine voice raged.

I choked for breath.

The weight of his body slammed the car door I had just opened. I remember looking at my surroundings for help. Cars passed without their drivers sensing my predicament. No people were in sight. Don't panic; panic can get you killed. The man led me toward the three steps into the park, spitting venom while poking a knife in my back. I have to do something–now. If I get in the park, I've had it. On the second step, I swung around and kicked him in the groin with my platform shoes. He fell to the ground, holding himself, rolling on the ground. I ran to the front of my apartment building, screaming to call the police. The front desk made the call, and the officers on duty arrived immediately.

"What happened, Baby?" asked one of the cops, Clifford, a guy I was going out with.

I met Clifford when I started representing a defendant in the DC Court in 1973. The woman I was defending had a record of solicitation cases. The defendant called me at home at 3:00 a.m. ranting and raving about hating lawyers, how she'd been in and out of jail on these charges before, and then confessed to me she was a man. He went into detail as to how he "hid" his genitals. His hostility scared me.

The following day, I asked the court for permission to withdraw from the case. My request was granted. I walked out of the courthouse, and the police officer who had been checking me out for months jumped in front of me and tackled the defendant inches from me. The vial of acid the defendant intended to throw in my face went on the leather of the officer's uniform and ate through it. Other officers swarmed and stripped Clifford's shirt off. I called my parents, and they said, "You don't need to be a lawyer; come home, remember the piano?" I invited Clifford to lunch as a thank you.

Clifford and I dated for several months until he pulled a gun on me. Like Dr. Jekyll, Clifford must have developed a secret potion to separate his personality's good and evil aspects. He could change into his increasingly dominant evil counterpart, Mr. Clifford Hyde.

The kind, protective Cliff Jekyll became jealous when I told him I wanted to see someone else. The lunatic Cliff Hyde decided if he couldn't have me, no one would have me. Why am I drawn to crazy people, and why are they drawn to me? Suffice it to say, I pressed charges against the man who assaulted me near the park. The case went to trial, and the assailant was convicted. I broke up with Clifford.

Marita became very protective of me after the assault. She didn't want me out of her sight. I checked on Marita daily to ensure she got to class on time, and she checked on me to ensure I was safe. Later, Marita moved to the Mount Pleasant neighborhood of Washington, DC.

Mt. Pleasant was a hip neighborhood with funky restaurants and shops. The area bordered Rock Creek Park and was densely urban. Marita and I attended many of the concerts by soon-to-be-famous people. We studied and partied together. We shopped and ate together.

Law school classes were painful. My spirit was broken. I seldom knew what was being discussed and prayed not to be called on. Watching the mouths of my professors didn't help me recognize the words they uttered. Visiting during office hours for help was a distant hope because I was too lost to know what to ask. I was intimidated, over my head, lost, stupid, and confused, in a new city with few friends.

WINNING THE BATTLE AGAINST MYSELF

I was losing the battle against myself. What made me think I was law school material? Not good enough, smart enough, and having all-too-human flaws made me too dumb to be a lawyer. At night I read and used my yellow highlighter at night until my head dropped into the book. Big Daddy and Big Momma sent a tape recorder to help me decipher the novel language. Were the professors speaking English? Feoffment... seisin ... unconscionable ...certiorari?

The recorder did not help. I had to get it together. I couldn't fail at this. I called my parents and suggested I get away for a couple of days to put my academics in a better perspective. My folks sent me a credit card, and I checked into a hotel in Bethesda, Maryland, for a week. I took my books with me. My friend Lee would call every night and read his notes to update me. Lee became a prominent labor lawyer. It was a good week because I could gather and put this new life in perspective. I centered myself.

Please make no mistake; when I returned to school, there was no epiphany — I was still totally lost. It was beyond dreadful.

Many other students had been marinated in the law and were there to carry on the family dynasty. While sitting outside during my second year, I noticed a limousine pulled up. David Eisenhower, former President Dwight Eisenhower's grandson and President Richard Nixon's current son-in-law, got out. The son of Brig. Gen. John Eisenhower, David spent the first half of his life around the U.S. presidency. David's grandfather, Dwight, the former president, was in Denver frequently when we were growing up because Mamie's (Dwight's wife) mother lived in Denver.

Mommy always knew when President Eisenhower came to Denver since she worked in the mayor's office. When the former president came, Vicki and I got to go to Mrs. Dowd's (Mamie's mother's) house because we were fortunate enough to have Secret Service and Denver police clearance. We were only 5 and 6, but President Eisenhower would give us our secret hand wave, which was waving with both hands. My classmate, David,

The Lost World

lived in the White House while attending GW and spent his time around some of the most influential people of the 20th century. The school that offered me the most money was the already monied and famous school. And it was for generational money and generational fame.

Boy, was I in the wrong place? A part of my legal education was a hands-on, intern-type approach. Visiting inmates at Lorton Reformatory Prison in Virginia was nerve-racking. It was for non-violent offenders serving short sentences. It was outdated and badly overcrowded. Cats prowled everywhere. All the inmates I saw were black. The cells and prison hallways were crumbling decay. The inmates shouted sexist comments and made lewd gestures toward me. All I could think was, thank God for jails.

I met Derrick Humphries in 1973, a guy who lived in a building adjacent to my New Hampshire Avenue apartment. He worked with Shirley Chisholm and the Congressional Black Caucus, an organization established in 1969 through which the concerns of black Americans reached Congress and how policy was delivered to disenfranchised communities. Derrick introduced me to Mrs. C, as I grew to call her. She was a bundle of energy with strong convictions. I got to know her when Derrick and I were hosts at the end of the September Congressional Black Caucus Dinner.

Later, she invited me to sit through the House of Representatives' role in the impeachment investigation of President Richard M. Nixon during the Watergate Scandal in the 1970s. The scandal stemmed from the Nixon administration's continual attempts to cover up its involvement in the June 17, 1972, break-in of the Democratic National Committee headquarters at the Washington, D.C. Watergate Office Building. There was a burglary and illegal wiretapping in the Watergate complex by President Richard Nixon's re-election campaign members. A subsequent break-in cover-up resulted in Nixon's resignation on August 9, 1974. What an opportunity for a law student.

WINNING THE BATTLE AGAINST MYSELF

I felt disappointment in those lawyers who perverted the profession I was in school to learn. Immediately after Watergate, I didn't think government experience was that important for our presidential candidates. Instead, I wanted authenticity and truth from a president. I now believe that government or political experience and technical knowledge of how our government bureaucracy works are essential in a president, as are authenticity, truth, legal acumen, business knowledge, management experience, and people skills.

The congressional pass from Shirley Chisholm permitted me to go to the Senate side of the Capitol to view the Senate Watergate hearings. I was proud to be one of the few Americans present when the first television broadcast from the Senate Chamber occurred at 10:00 p.m. on December 19, 1974, to swear in the new vice president. Thus, the public caught a fleeting glimpse of the Senate Chamber, but the cameras were removed once that swearing-in ceremony ended. Little did I know it would be my destiny to usher in daily televised Senate proceedings twelve years later, in 1986, as Deputy Sergeant at Arms of the U.S. Senate.

On January 25, 1972, Shirley Chisholm, the first black woman elected to the United States Congress, announced her candidacy for president. The Congressional Black Caucus refused to endorse her candidacy, which she helped found the previous year. The reason? Some in the Congressional Black Caucus thought Mrs. C's focus on gender and outreach to other groups subverted the Caucus's mission and its explicit focus on race. I related to Mrs. C's betrayal by the Congressional Black Caucus because of the CSU Black Student Alliance, which I co-founded, betrayal with its refusal to nominate me for Homecoming Queen.

Because of my horrific law school experience, I was beaming with pride to have, after 233 years, the first black woman on the highest court in the land, Associate Justice Ketanji Brown Jackson. The Supreme Court decides cases that affect our

The Lost World

lives. On Thursday, April 7, 2022, I recall watching the 53-47 Senate vote to confirm her nomination. And, to make the great moment more extraordinary, the first woman and first black Vice President of the United States, Honorable Kamala Harris, presided over the vote. Justice Jackson made the court relevant to all our citizens. Her experience representing low-income defendants was a first in the court. The high court was starting to look like America.

I made time for socializing despite my studies. Aside from a friendship with Derrick Humphries in 1973, I formed a business relationship with Claude Roxborough in early 1974. Both of these men, attorneys, were visionary entrepreneurs. Claude and I spent much of our time discussing plans for a nightclub that appealed to sophisticated, exclusive, educated, middle-class young blacks. The plans and resources came together, and The Foxtrappe opened in 1975. The club hosted famous athletes, entertainers, politicians, and people like me.

My not-forever-love sent me plane tickets to fly to some of his games. I was glad to leave Washington for a few days. I deluded myself into taking law books, promising to study on planes and during downtime. I never opened the books.

Our lives were so different. He was a professional athlete who was a star. I was a law student who was in over her head. He had a luxury apartment; I had lived in a roach-infested dormitory. After games, gorgeous women with designer clothes and expertly applied make-up lined the hallways, waiting for the athletes to exit the dressing rooms. I stood with them in my jeans and sweatshirts, feeling insecure. Back at his apartment, I cooked breakfast for his friends and dinner for us. Despite his fame, we enjoyed simple things like snuggling on the couch and watching television.

In November 1974, Big Daddy died at age 83. I got a call in late October to come home because Big Daddy was very ill. My parents picked me up at the airport, and we went directly to the hospital in case something happened in the interim. Big

WINNING THE BATTLE AGAINST MYSELF

Daddy had never been in the hospital in my lifetime; I thought he would get well and go home like I did many times after being hospitalized. A hospital is not a place where you die. You go there, get well, and go home.

Big Daddy was larger than life; death wouldn't mess with him.

When I saw him in his hospital bed, he said to me, "Hi, Little Girl! Did they tell you I was going to die?"

I said, "Of course not, Big Daddy. No one told me you were going to die."

Then he said, "You took time out of your law studies to come to see about me?"

I said, "Yes, Sir, of course!" Our conversation was matter-of-fact, as always. No tears were shed. Big Daddy must have known the truth, but no one ever told me he would die.

Big Daddy died. Vicki called and told me. She said she entered Big Daddy's hospital room while he took his last breath. She rolled a towel and put it under his chin because his mouth fell open. Nurses came in, removed the towel from his chin, and put Big Daddy's bridge in his mouth. I wasn't exactly sure what a bridge was, but knowing about a bridge in a mouth didn't seem necessary. Then Vicki said she put the towel back under his chin.

All I could do was make airline reservations. I was numb; I couldn't cry. I packed my clothes and headed for the airport. Vicki picked me up at the airport, and we went straight home. There was a roped-off area for us to park in front of the house. Coming home again, where my grandfather's picture was on the front page of both major newspapers, was overwhelming. Cars flooded our neighborhood, with their occupants bringing food and flowers. Big Daddy was Santa Claus to everyone. He was the one who would always give you a fair shake. He was invincible. I thought he'd always be around.

I didn't think I'd have this hole in my life. The funeral plan had been to have black and white musicians in a parade playing

The Lost World

When the Saints Go Marching In. Big Daddy had founded and merged the black and white musician unions into Musicians Local 623. They couldn't play the song outside because of the rain.

On the way to Shorter A.M.E. Church in the funeral procession on a cold, dreary, wet day, people lined the streets for blocks. When we arrived at the church, people were everywhere. Vicki and I had never seen a funeral gathering of this magnitude. We exited the limousine, and a group of men pushed the crowd back to make a path for us to enter the church. The overflow room and balcony were full, and the chairs they had set up in the gymnasium were full. It appeared that 90% of blacks in Denver attended. A tape recording of him playing his music during the service was difficult to listen to.

Hearing Big Daddy play the violin at his own funeral triggered memories of a great man whom death had silenced. My mind's eye had trouble reconciling my grandfather's love of music with the dead man in a coffin with fingers that would never again play the music I was hearing. A large choir sang, and musicians played string instruments. The governor, mayor, state senators, and old and new friends spoke. The funeral service was a very long spectacle.

After the service, well-wishers, including dignitaries, rushed us to the point of dizzying. It wasn't very comforting. Food was served in the gymnasium, the repast. The motorcade to the cemetery was long, inconveniencing drivers caught unexpectedly. When we arrived, people who hadn't been able to get into the church for the ceremony stood outside in the rain at the cemetery. Since the family was at the front of the funeral procession, we had to stand graveside in the cold rain, waiting for over 80 cars to arrive.

Big Momma didn't go to any of this. She had suffered a stroke, and we feared it would be too much for her. Big Daddy's face appears on a Colorado Panorama: A People's History, a two-block-long tile mural on the southeast side of the Colorado Convention Center. George Morrison, Sr. Park is a beautiful

WINNING THE BATTLE AGAINST MYSELF

urban linear park near downtown Denver. It is across the street from a school where Daddy was the principal.

Big Daddy's death got more problematic for me as time passed, not at the moment. The older I get, the more I realize his impact on my life. It's taken years for me to climb out of his enormous footprint. When you're in the footprint, you don't realize you're in it because you can't see the sides of it until you get to its perimeter, and you see that part goes up, so you must be in a footprint, but you wander around in it for decades before you know it's a footprint.

I was the only black law student accepted nationwide in a criminal justice program at Georgetown University. How on earth did that happen? Leaving Washington, DC, for Colorado twice, once before Big Daddy died and again for his funeral, in this selective program, didn't sit well with the program leaders. The program lasted for one semester. I was placed in the States Attorney's Office in Rockville, Maryland. I was the second chair at trials and wrote briefs. The lawyer I worked with left me alone in the courtroom, but I never ratted him out. So much for justice for those defendants.

When there was a 20-year reunion, I wasn't invited. And I was pretty famous by then. Allan, whom I met in the 1974 program, flew in from California for the reunion and insisted I go with him. I went. The leaders of the program shunned me. They were still upset with me for my two trips to Colorado that caused me to miss a substantial portion of the program.

Still struggling through law school after losing my grandfather, being ostracized in the Georgetown program, surviving an acid catastrophe, and breaking up with a deranged cop, I was trying to find my niche in the law, but it continually didn't fit.

As an undergrad, I got interested in criminal law; that interest stayed with me through law school, and that's when I was admitted to the national criminal justice program at Georgetown, where the leaders hated me because of my two Colorado trips; after law school, I still thought I wanted to

The Lost World

be in criminal law, so I worked as a prosecutor with a licensed lawyer who left me in a criminal trial without regard for justice for the defendant and as a defense attorney who'd narrowly missed having acid thrown in her face. I had an aptitude for it, but it wasn't floating in my boat. I needed to make a change.

Chapter 9

Home Again

"You leave home to seek your fortune and, when you get it, you go home and share it with your family."

-Anita Baker

After stints in the District of Columbia courts and Maryland's States' Attorney's Office, I returned to Denver in 1978. Both of my grandmothers were ill, and my folks needed my help. My parents rented an apartment in the same building where Vicki lived, the Piccadilly Apartments in Glendale, south of where I grew up. I lived on the third floor; Vicki lived on the first floor. We put food, medicine, and clothes on the elevator and sent them up or down to each other.

Everything traveled via the elevator: more Marinara sauce, please, medication for menstrual cramps, send the pink pajamas, need the black patent shoes with the 3" heel, do you have the prescription medication? I'll wait for the garlic bread, okra, rice, pork chops, neck bones, Sugar Babies, greens and cornbread, wigs, and shampoo. It was fun getting acquainted with my sister again as a fellow adult.

I met a guy who asked me out for the coming weekend. The Piccadilly parking lot was concave, which meant trouble climbing the hill without snow tires or chains in the winter. I

Home Again

warned this guy I would go out with on Friday of the importance of getting snow tires or chains. Friday evening came. He picked me up at my apartment. As we approached the parking lot, the fluffy early evening snow was getting heavier, and the pavement was slippery. When he tried to navigate the parking lot hill, the tires spun; there was no traction. I told him, "This is what happens when you procrastinate."

He asked, "What does procrastinate mean?"

At this point, all I could do was leave. I calmly exited the car, said nothing, walked back into my apartment building, and never answered his calls.

I asked Vicki if she had seen Ronnie, my teenage crush. "No, I haven't seen him, but heard he went to Vietnam."

"What?! Is he back here ... in Denver? Is he married?"

"I don't know. I'll ask Carl the next time I talk to him."

"Doesn't Kearney still live here? He'd know how to reach Ronnie."

"Kearney wouldn't tell me even if he knew."

"Why not?"

"He's strange. I don't know how to reach him anyway."

The Vietnam War went from November 1, 1955, to April 30, 1975. Direct U.S. involvement ended in 1973. China became communist in 1949, and communists controlled North Vietnam. The U.S. feared communism would spread to South Vietnam and the rest of Asia. It sent money, supplies, and military advisers to help the South Vietnamese Government. Independence, freedom, and liberation were the primary objectives of the South Vietnamese.

The U.S. committed 550,000 troops to the Vietnam front at the height of the conflict, suffered over 58,000 casualties, and engaged in battle after battle with communist forces until its withdrawal in 1973. Having lost friends in the war, I was grateful to God for bringing Ronnie safely home.

One night, Vicki and I wanted green chili from the bar across the parking lot. I volunteered to go. It was 1979 when

WINNING THE BATTLE AGAINST MYSELF

Roots 2 The Next Generation continued a 21-hour television miniseries that traced author Alex Haley's family back to an enslaved African, Kunta Kinte and told the story of his family's growth in America. At age 15, Kunta Kinte's daughter, Kizzy, was sold to Tom Lea, who raped her, resulting in the birth of their son, who Tom Lea also owned as an enslaved person.

There were nothing but cowboys in the bar — loud and drunk. One guy said, "Looky here, we have Kizzy with us! I want a piece of that."

Others said, "We'd all like a piece of that ass."

The cowboy bartender whispered, "I think you ought to get out of here..."

I ran back to the apartment as fast as I could. I locked all the doors behind me. I told Vicki what had happened, and we pledged never to return to that place.

It was the 70s and Vicki and I got caught up in the pot culture. Our experimentation did not go well. After an evening of indulging, we decided we needed more munchies. My sister took the wheel, and we headed to a grocery store that was two blocks away. This was the night there was a national blackout. Somehow, we ended up on railroad tracks, miles from our apartment.

By Grace, we found our way back to the grocery store. I got out as my sister stared ahead, clutching the steering wheel. I approached the entrance and stepped on the footbed. The door did not open.

I stepped on the pad again. It would not open. I put my foot on the pad, lifted it off, placed it down again, and lifted it; the door had to be broken. An employee observer came out of the store and said, "Follow me. I know what you want."

I followed him without question.

The employee observer got a basket, and I walked behind him. He went down several aisles, and I followed him. He was in the checkout line, and I stood next to him. He finally spoke, "Do you have any money? May I get some money from your purse to pay for this?"

Home Again

My tongue was too heavy to move. He paid for the groceries, put the change in my purse, and walked me to one of the four cars in the parking lot. My sister was still clinging to the steering wheel, eyes blankly staring ahead.

"Be safe," the kind, probable pothead, stranger said. Vicki and I sat in the car eating Cheetos, potato chips, cookies, ice cream bars, and candy. Somehow, we got home. We found orange fingerprints on the car door and windows the following morning. We also found an empty rectangular baking dish in the sink. Pie crumbs were on the counter. Peach cans were in the trash can. We did not remember baking or eating an entire peach cobbler.

Vicki got me into another mess and left me hanging. This time, it was at American National Bank. She asked me to drive her to her bank. We came from a Sangria-Mexican food lunch, smoked a joint, and now Vicki remembered she had to go to the bank.

There were yet to be any drive-through banks. I maneuvered the ramps that wound around like Lombard Street in San Francisco inside the bank parking structure. We walked into the bank and headed to the counter to fill out forms.

Vicki looked up and saw an armed guard. She was high and worried that the guard would figure it out. She got paranoid, froze, stiffened, eyes blank, and walked like a robot to the elevator.

Vicki said nothing to me. The elevator went down. I knew I had to get out of the bank, especially considering I was a lawyer who had imbibed an illegal substance. Also, I was too ripped to be in a bank with an armed guard, a stoned sister who had left like a zombie, and no bank business.

I started speaking loudly, saying, "Oh, I left my money in the car." Could I have been more obvious?

I couldn't stop talking. I scribbled nonsense on blank bank paper to distract others from noticing me. My dry mouth started again, and I loudly continued, "Why is the elevator taking so long? Oh, machines, you can't do anything with them or without them."

I tried to be cool — what a tell. I rode the elevator down to the parking lot where Vicki was loitering in the parking garage, looking suspicious with glassy eyes. I demanded an explanation for her behavior, and she offered fragmented gibberish that made no sense.

My mother got me a job at Gorsuch, Kirgis, Campbell, Walker & Grover. Mommy first met Mr. Campbell in 1947 when he was Denver Mayor Quigg Newton's Manager of Safety. They served together on the 2nd Judicial Nominating Commission from 1971 to 1977. Mr. Campbell was a giant of a man — in size (6'2") and generosity. He was called "The Dean of Colorado Lawyers." Curiously, I was the only black in any role in the firm then. I helped write briefs on tax, civil rights, labor, eminent domain, and contract law — but no criminal law. Once again, I was losing the battle against myself. Where did I belong?

The law firm was similar to successfully getting onto the beach at Normandy on D-Day, securing the beachhead but still needing to get across France to Berlin. Maybe going back to criminal law would ground me. A friend, Norm Early, Deputy Denver District Attorney, persuaded me to come to the Denver District Attorney's Office.

After I left the Gorsuch law firm, they hired Wiley Daniel, who became a Federal judge, Chair of the Federal Judge's Association, and co-founder of the Judicial Resources Committee's Diversity Subcommittee of the Judicial Conference of the United States. Most importantly, Wiley was one of my dearest friends. I think of him every day.

I ran into Ronnie, my teenage crush, near the law firm. "Hi," he said.

"Hi, how are you?" I asked.

"I'm ok," he said. We stood there looking at the ground.

"You look great, Ronnie."

"You always look great."

Home Again

Why didn't I say more? Why didn't he say more?

Vicki told me Ronnie had joined the Air Force after Vietnam and was working as a glazer, a glass cutter. I occasionally saw him in a peach-colored suit near the law firm on 17th Street. He was handsome. I don't understand what happened to us.

Years later, Ronnie told me he would go home and change his work clothes into his one suit — the peach-colored one.

We said hello when we saw each other and went in opposite directions. Ronnie was painfully shy and couldn't find his voice. I should have caught on. One day, he gave me his phone number. I never called him. Vicki told me Ronnie lived with someone before I came home. My hope was shattered again.

The District Attorney's Office wasn't the professional answer for me either. I thought I was a good writer, but Brooke Wunnicke told me otherwise. Brooke was Chief Deputy of Appeals in the Denver District Attorney's Office. I resented her critique of my writing. Who was she, and what had she done in life to judge me? The unmitigated gall.

After I put my ego in storage, I heralded her brilliance and was honored to have her as a mentor.

Brooke overcame countless gender-based boundaries and was instrumental in mentoring attorneys, paving the way for female attorneys, and improving society's legal field. Another of her mentees, Ralph, and his wife had a baby boy with cancer. I went to Children's Hospital with Ralph every day. I was there when the baby died. It was an experience I will never forget.

Nothing was happening in my career. I thought I'd try criminal justice administration. My mother found a job opening at the State Department of Criminal Justice. I disclosed to Dale Tooley, the District Attorney, and Norm Early, his deputy, that I was applying for the state job. The state process was long. I had to take a test and qualify through a complicated, bureaucratic, nonsensical process. There was a criminal background check, four levels of interviews: personnel director, employees, deputy director, then director, and writing exercises.

Meanwhile, I found out there was an opening for Chair of the Colorado Civil Rights Commission—a dream job my father held—so I decided to apply. The selection committee included the second black teacher I had in Junior High, a family friend, and a member of our church, Regis Groff. The odds were looking good. I sailed through the bureaucratic process and became one of two finalists.

My final interview with Commission members was impressive. I felt that the position would be offered. It wasn't. I didn't get the job. I got two phone calls: one from a white Republican woman and one from a white Democrat man, both of whom were on the selection committee. They both asked that I consider their call confidential. The woman wanted me to know that the committee vote was unanimous in my favor, except for Regis Groff, who said he couldn't vote for a Republican. The man said that Mr. Groff had clarified that he couldn't support a Republican even though I was "exceptionally qualified." Regis Groff, my second black teacher, family friend, and parishioner, had betrayed me.

Colorado State Government

I finally heard back from the Colorado Division of Criminal Justice. I got the job. It turned out to be a nightmare. My job was administering and monitoring block grants to law enforcement agencies throughout the state under the Law Enforcement Assistance Administration (LEAA). The LEAA was responsible for administering Federal funding to state and local law enforcement agencies. I selected cities and townships across the state whose law enforcement departments needed training, salary increases, and career development. For example, although outdated, the grants I administered gave police departments the ability to transmit pictures of precarious situations from the ground or helicopter to command headquarters.

Home Again

Half a block from my job, I spent time at the state capital with legislators who served on a criminal justice sub-committee. My boss, Diane, despised me and watched me like a hawk. Maybe she thought I was stealing government property or something. I didn't try to win her acceptance because I didn't like or respect her authority. One reason for her disdain was what I did to enhance an upcoming meeting with the Colorado Division of Criminal Justice governing board. Diane sent invitations to LEAA Washington staff to invite them to keynote a Denver luncheon. It would have been a feather in her cap if she could bring in a LEAA national staffer. I knew the top man at LEAA who presided over the country, Homer Broome.

I met Homer Broome in Washington at a criminal law symposium in law school when he was one of the original charter members of the National Organization of Black Law Enforcement Executives. We stayed in touch, and in 1978, Homer was nominated by President Jimmy Carter and confirmed by the Senate to become Administrator of the LEAA, part of the Department of Justice, in Washington, DC. When I called him regarding the Colorado board meeting keynote speech, Mr. Broome immediately accepted. Homer praised my professionalism, work ethic, and dedication to the criminal justice profession during his speech. He also waxed eloquently about my glowing national reputation as a trusted adviser to other high-ranking Department of Justice officials. Diane turned green. Her face gnarled, and her lips curled. My action was immature and petty, but I enjoyed it anyway. Later, when the Colorado staff lauded me, Diane told a fellow employee, "Trudi isn't all she claims to be." Whatever that meant.

I saw Ronnie on the street several times while working at the Division of Criminal Justice. I was at one of the lowest points in my life. Ronnie was a ray of sunshine, but from my perspective, he didn't display interest in me. I wish he had given me any sign—any hint—that he cared. I was confused, lonely, and miserable. I needed someone to help me through life. I would have been his for the asking. He didn't ask.

Mary Estill Buchanan, Colorado Secretary of State and head of the criminal justice subcommittee, called to commend me on an article I wrote. We made plans for lunch. That luncheon led to many others and a burgeoning friendship.

In the Fall of 1980, Mary Estill invited me to a cocktail party at her home. I immediately went shopping. At Neusteters department store, I bought the most expensive dress I had owned up to that point. Neusteters was considered the leading women's wear retailer outside of New York. The dress was cream-colored with a boat neckline and drop shoulders, long pleated sleeves tapered at the wrist, and a pleated skirt. I kept the dress, and it still fits.

At the cocktail party, I was introduced to the big-time Colorado Republicans. Neil Bush was the first person I met at Mary Estill's soiree. Neil was the son of future President H.W. Bush and the brother of future President W. Bush. Neil was charming and funny.

I met Joe and Holly Coors of Coors Brewery at Mary Estill's party. Joe would become a member of President Reagan's "kitchen cabinet." The "kitchen cabinet" comprised conservative businessmen who served as unofficial advisers to the President. Kitchen cabinet members were Joseph Coors, President of the Coors Brewing Company, and the Council for National Policy founder. He invested the initial $250,000 in seed money to start the Heritage Foundation in 1973. The Heritage Foundation was a conservative think-tank to formulate and promote public policies based on free enterprise, limited government, individual freedom, traditional American values, and strong national defense.

Thomas Roe was a businessman and industrialist from Greenville, South Carolina. He was chairman of Builder Marts of America, Inc.; Edwin Meese III, a wealthy California attorney, was a prominent adviser in the Administration and worked

Home Again

under Governor Reagan in California. He was appointed the 75th Attorney General of the United States; Justin Dart, an American businessman, was considered the "boy wonder" of the drug store industry. He was a leader in the disability rights movement for three decades and an advocate for the rights of women, people of color, and gays and lesbians. William A. Wilson, a wealthy Los Angeles businessman who was appointed the first U.S. Ambassador to the Vatican; Holmes Tuttle, a wealthy California businessman and auto dealer whose son, Robert Holmes Tuttle, worked in the White House under President Reagan and was later Ambassador to the U.K. during George W. Bush's second term; and William French Smith, who served first as Ronald Reagan's lawyer in California and then accompanied him to Washington as the 74th Attorney General of the United States. I found it hard to admire these men because I figured that anyone who had their kind of money had lied, cheated, and stolen from someone else throughout the generations. I believed that the path to riches was seldom pure.

Other new acquaintances at the cocktail party were Anne Gorsuch, mother of future Associate Justice of the U.S. Supreme Court Neil Gorsuch (who was about seventeen years younger than me), wife of David Gorsuch, and daughter-in-law of John Gorsuch, both of the law firm I worked in, Gorsuch, Kirgis, Campbell, Walker and Grover, and who became head of the Environmental Protection Agency under President Reagan; Bob Burford, who became head of the Bureau of Land Management under President Reagan and married Annie Gorsuch in 1981; Phil Winn, Chairman of the Colorado Republican Party, who would become Federal Housing Commissioner and later, Ambassador to Switzerland under President Reagan; and Bill Armstrong, U. S. Senator (R-CO). This was the Colorado Republican connection; it was masterful networking, if I say so myself.

My friendship with Annie Gorsuch was unrelated to my tenure at Gorsuch, Kirgis, Campbell, Walker, and Grover. I met her in a political setting a few years after leaving the law firm. Annie was strikingly beautiful. She had black hair and wore furs and jewels. Always impeccably groomed, she could charm the most ardent curmudgeon. Annie's sense of humor left me in stitches. I loved her self-confidence, despite those who tried to dampen it. She was eight years older than me, but we had much in common. Foremost, our love of food, especially pizza and beer.

During my 17-year tenure at the Administrative Office of the United States Courts, one highlight was the day Neil Gorsuch came before me for his judge orientation. I asked if he was related to Annie; he replied she was his mother and had passed away; heartbroken, I commiserated and eventually remembered my job of orienting new judges to the Federal judiciary. I closed by stating how proud his mother would be of his success and how proud I was to sit before him on that occasion.

With high-level networking, you have to be appropriate. I was an easy sell for the Republicans. I came to the table with the "right" pedigree, the "right" educational degrees from the "right" schools, the "right" way to behave in public, the "right" looks, and the "right" demeanor. When they put themselves out there, these power-brokers had to be secure in their knowledge of their ingénue. Their credibility was on the line, so they had to be confident that I wouldn't embarrass them.

When I recommended people or hired them for jobs, I wanted them to fit that same criterion. If you make an ass of yourself, you make an ass of me. You can have the stars aligned for you, but lose them through inappropriate behavior. You can go too far. You cannot cross a line because if you do, you won't get back in—no second chances. You have to bring all these things to the table but wait for the people at the table to come to you.

"Mommy, you've told me for years that our family has been Republicans for five generations. Why is that? What is the history of our people in that political party?" I asked.

Home Again

"We've talked about President Lincoln signing the Emancipation Proclamation, and since the era of Reconstruction, Negroes were in the party of Lincoln. These black Republicans are not new; they are just newly visible."

"That's true. It seems like I see more black Republicans talking on TV than I used to. Does that mean there is a changing level of support among black voters?"

"Individual black Republicans are more visible within and better supported by the GOP, but the Republican Party itself is not gaining votes among ordinary black Americans. While it was once advantageous to hide black Republicans from the view of white voters, it is now strategic to elevate black Republicans to visible positions within the party. The goal of bringing these black faces to the foreground is not to increase the share of black votes but to signal to moderate white voters that the party is not racist. The distinction is subtle but crucial."

My family never left the Republican Party. I was able to see the intersection of race and politics. Issues such as capitalism, less regulation, limited government, and low taxes appealed to my sense of an individualistic approach to societal problems. The exception to my individualistic approach was the institutional racism and sexism prevalent in many of our laws. As you will read later, this exception became my White House portfolio. I firmly believed that having representation in both political parties was critical to including blacks in policy- and decision-making on concerns affecting our nation.

When forming the Colorado Black Republican Council, I knew a few blacks who were Republican, even those hiding in the closet. And my mother knew quite a few more ... the older ones. I started sending them letters, notices, and invitations about events at Republican headquarters. I even got some converts, not to the party, but to action and participation. I informed them that I supported George H. W. Bush in the 1980 primary, Neil's father, and that the Council also needed those who supported Ronald Reagan.

WINNING THE BATTLE AGAINST MYSELF

As a fifth-generation Republican, I was aware of the history of blacks in the Republican Party. In fact, from the 41st Congress (1869-1871) to the 74th Congress (1935-1937), all 45 black members of Congress were Republicans. After the 15th Amendment to the U.S. Constitution was passed in 1870, allowing most of the black males in the former Confederate states to vote, the Republican Party got the votes of a majority of black Americans, prompting Frederick Douglass, a nineteenth-century Colored abolitionist who escaped from slavery and then risked his freedom by becoming an outspoken anti-slavery lecturer, writer, and publisher, to remark that for them, "The Republican Party was the ship and all else was the sea."

Ronald Reagan was inaugurated in January 1981. Phil Winn, whom I met at Mary Estill Buchanan's (Colorado Secretary of State) party in 1980, was head of the Colorado Republican Party in 1980, and I founded the Colorado Black Republican Council in 1980. In that capacity, I made an out-of-state ally who was part of the California Black Republican Council, Clarence Thomas. Clarence and I became buddies in 1981 when we were both in the Reagan Administration in Washington. He was exceptionally astute, always informed, humble, and downright humorous. Clarence made me laugh out loud. He was a loyal friend. Clarence later became an Associate Justice of the United States Supreme Court.

I had top-level positions in the Reagan Administration, which was the executive branch of the Federal government, from 1981 to 1985 (U.S. Department of Housing and Urban Development, U.S. Department of Health and Human Services, and the White House), from 1985 to 1987, in the U.S. Senate (Deputy Sergeant at Arms), the legislative branch of the Federal government. From 1987 to 1990 (Member of Council, Administrative Conference of the United States). The bulk of my career was in the Federal government's judicial branch for 17 years at the Administrative Office of the United States Courts. All the jobs were in Washington, DC, except one in Denver.

Home Again

Executive Branch of the Federal Government

When the Senate confirmed Phil Winn, head of the Colorado Republican Party, as Federal Housing Commissioner in the U.S. Department of Housing and Urban Development (HUD) in March 1981, he insisted I join him as Deputy Assistant Secretary for Policy and Budget. Phil and I had established mutual trust, respect, and friendship. He liked my passion, honesty, efficiency, and power of persuasion. If something couldn't be done, I'd tell him; I would also tell him when I thought he was wrong.

One of my friends was Dorothy Height, President of the National Council of Negro Women for 40 years. She was the most influential woman in the modern civil rights movement. She fought for equal rights for both blacks and women. Dr. Height supported women's rights before the male leadership of the civil rights movement joined that fight. She engaged all women, regardless of race, in the struggle for equality for blacks, even as some women's groups continued to discriminate. Dr. Height was awarded the Presidential Medal of Freedom in 1994 and the Congressional Gold Medal in 2004 for her civil rights activism. What a grand, dignified, and beautiful lady she was. Her presence in any setting was a joy to behold, with hats to match every outfit. And she loved me. We'd enjoy tea in her Southwest apartment near the wharf in D.C.

Infertility became the next problem. I was forty-two years old. I learned for the first time that one of my two fallopian tubes had been closed since birth. Fibroids in my uterus blocked my fallopian tube, affecting fertility. Fertility drugs to stimulate ovulation didn't work. I had three laparoscopic surgeries, a hysteroscopy, and a myomectomy. Intrauterine insemination was too expensive. By God's Grace, Logan was born in 1992. My life priorities immediately changed: how to keep him healthy; how to provide him the best education available; how to guard his safety against police brutality; how to give him the moral imagination to achieve and thrive; how to encourage his spiritual wellness; and how to ensure his respect for all people.

WINNING THE BATTLE AGAINST MYSELF

By 1995, infection in my lady parts made me deathly ill. My parents flew me to Denver, where I had an emergency hysterectomy. The surgery was scheduled for one to two hours. My surgery lasted seven hours, during which my appendix burst, prompting a physician from Colorado Springs to fly into Denver to save me. I flat-lined. I was hospitalized for eight days. The Colorado Springs doctor later told me my situation was "grave." At age 45, the complete hysterectomy threw me into menopause since my ovaries were also removed.

Health issues didn't give me a break that year. In December 1995, a lump was found in my breast. A biopsy revealed a calcification that was non-cancerous. Waiting for the laboratory to examine the tissue for cancer cells was agonizing, the most challenging part of the ordeal.

Chapter 10

Lunch with Holly

> "I wanted the young African-American girls also on the bus to know that they had a right to be there because they had paid their fare just like the white passengers."
>
> **-Claudette Colvin**
> **Rosa Park's inspiration**

A Brown Palace Hotel luncheon with Holly Coors of Coors Brewery fame changed my career trajectory forever. Located in the heart of Denver, the Brown had stained-glass skylights, Florentine arches, and intricate iron panels. It was an icon, rich in tradition and history. Its halls had been grazed by celebrities and politicians alike, including President Reagan in 1981.

We ate our salads, drank tea, and shared a sinful slice of five-layer yellow cake with buttercream frosting. As we drank more tea, I told Holly I would like to return to Washington.

Holly said, "Really? I want to create a little White House. I want to do what Nancy (Reagan) is doing at the White House."

"What do you mean?" I asked.

She said, "The way she and Ted are freshening up the second-and third-floor private quarters."

"Ted who and what's going on with the private quarters?" I asked.

"Ted Graber, the movie actor turned decorator. Beverly Hills and Hollywood adore him. You know the private quarters, Trudi–the Yellow Room, the Treaty Room, the Lincoln Bedroom, and the Queens' Bedroom," she replied.

I asked, "Why would you think I'd know something like that, Holly?"

"Oh, my! We must get you in the White House," she exclaimed.

"Yeah, but I'm absolutely sure I won't be invited to the private quarters. I want to work there, not sleep there," I clarified.

Ignoring what I said, Holly enthused, "Their bedroom is glorious. The walls are covered in hand-painted, 18th-century-style Chinese paper. Nancy is trying to restore everything. I hear it was a mess when they moved in. I hope the press doesn't get a hold of her efforts. They'll destroy her."

I was silent.

Holly gulped, "Do you think they'll find out about the 4,370 pieces of crimson china she's ordered?"

I asked, "Who's they? Are you talking about the media?"

She answered, "Yes."

"Of course, they'll find out. If you know, they already know. I don't care about this kind of stuff. I want to work there to see if I can block some of the policies that negatively impact minorities," I said.

She mentioned, "I don't know about his policies. That's Joe's territory."

"Umm."

"So, you want to work at the White House? It was more of a statement than a question. Let me explore a bit."

"Okay. Let's dive into that cake."

We laughed as we stabbed the cake with our forks.

Most of my friends were back east, and I missed the flair for melodramas. I enjoyed taking the quiet car of an Amtrak

Lunch with Holly

train from Washington's Union Station to New York's Penn Station, with its suffocating smell, for luncheons, shopping, and off-Broadway productions.

Within a week of lunch with Holly, I received a call from the White House to come for an interview. A lightweight white linen suit, a fuchsia blouse, and comfortable sandals purchased for the occasion, I was ready to face Washington, DC's unbearable summer humidity and heat.

I took a taxi from National Airport to the Hay Adams Hotel, across from Lafayette Park and the White House. The Hay Adams was an elegant, plush hotel. My tiny room was charming, with a lovely view of the White House. I made a dinner reservation at the Old Ebbitt Grill, a block from the White House because I knew it would be impossible to get in the same night of my arrival without one. Ebbitt Grill was Washington's oldest bar and restaurant. I had been there a couple of times before. My favorite seating area was Grant's Bar at the rear of the restaurant adjacent to the Atrium Dining Room. The room boasted a ceiling mural and oil paintings.

The following day, my anticipation was palatable. I walked through the White House gate and became strangely aware of my feet. They seemed like size 15, and my footfalls sounded unnaturally loud. I presented my credentials at a small security booth to a guard with a clipboard. I watched his eyes scan the list of names with my breath held. Relief flooded my veins when he found my name and let me pass. I'd imagined being thrown to the ground with a body cavity search.

After all, this was the Reagan White House, and I was black and female. Reagan was alleged to view black women as "welfare queens" and promiscuous. I considered him someone who wrapped his racism in a paternal façade. Even while knowing this, I continued. I'd come this far and didn't want to slam the door on an opportunity. I'd possibly been given a chance to work in a place built by enslaved people. In this house, Abraham Lincoln blended reconciliation and justice when he signed the

WINNING THE BATTLE AGAINST MYSELF

Emancipation Proclamation, and I was walking into the place where I could make a difference. Questions tumbled through my mind as I made my way in. Is making a difference an outdated cliché? Would I consider it? Would I pass it up because of the current occupant in the White House?

I crossed the half-moon driveway into a double door opened by military personnel in impeccable uniforms. My first stop was the West Wing sitting room. I sat in one of the old chairs with sagging seats and worn arms. My nerves blocked out; insecurity began taking over. I didn't even know who I'd be meeting with at this point!

Five excruciating, self-doubting minutes later, an escort came for me.

"Where are we headed?" I asked with my voice too high-pitched.

"To your meeting," he said, maintaining his brisk walk, eyes straight forward.

"I know, but who am I meeting with?"

He stopped unexpectedly. I nearly ran into his back, and turned. "They didn't tell you?"

"No." I forced my hands to stay at my sides and not wring with nerves.

"That's odd." After a half-shrug, he turned and continued walking briskly.

We had no more conversation. I glanced at the offices as we walked, amazed at their tiny size. Looking out the window, I saw a lawn with 45° angle stripes, leaving that freshly mowed meticulous look.

Faith Ryan Whittlesey's office was in the West Wing Colonnade. We stopped at her long, narrow, sparsely furnished office. Faith was Ambassador to Switzerland before directing the White House Office of Public Liaison.

I sat in a chair across from her desk, ready to impress. She didn't make eye contact, seemed exhausted and distracted, and kept looking at her watch. She asked only a few questions. My

Lunch with Holly

excitement dissipated with each passing minute. I felt put off. I got the impression that Faith was box-ticking:

- Black—check
- Female—check
- Educated—check
- Presentable—check
- Articulate—check

I wanted to be anywhere but there. Faith suddenly hopped up and motioned for me to follow her. My jaw dropped. I was sure she was kicking me out of the White House. She must not have known I was black, and now I was being kicked out of the Reagan White House because of my race. Typical bigotry. Expected humiliation. At least I had comfortable shoes on for my mortifying return to the hotel.

To my surprise, my journey had just begun.

Another surprise was the size of the Oval Office, which turned out to be much smaller than I envisioned, with three windows behind the Resolute desk and a fireplace.

The President was standing next to it. He smiled at me. I was standing at the threshold of the French doors with trembling hands, a racing heart, and sweat patches forming under my arms. The credenza was filled with family pictures. Two chairs flanked the desk with cream-colored upholstery. Two-facing Queen Anne chairs with yellow damask upholstery complemented the white fireplace. An array of antique hydrangeas, ranunculus roses, and greenery flanked a long table. A few petals had fallen onto the table. The oval rug was pale blue with gold designs, flowers, and blue stars. The room was tastefully understated, not flashy.

The President approached me, left arm extended. His size stunned me. So overwhelmed, I couldn't raise my arm to meet his outstretched one. Images seemed to show him writing right-handed, not left-handed, adding to my inability to think clearly or quickly. President Reagan was tall and broad. He was a handsome man. I didn't want to look too hard as I remembered my overdeveloped imagination about what the marine at The White House door might have thought.

And where did Faith go? I thought she was behind me.

The President wore a brown suit and an ivory shirt, and his hair was dark. It looked natural. It wasn't like Rudy Giuliani's black dye running down his face. His cheeks were naturally red-rouged.

Looking into the President's eyes snapped me out of my stupor. They were compassionate, actually playful eyes. Reagan seemed intensely human. He made direct eye contact throughout our brief encounter. It was a penetrating contact. Perhaps the President was experiencing hearing loss. I recalled that same piercing look from my grandfather and father, who had impaired hearing. They both became masters of lip reading. But I hadn't heard anything about the President's hearing on the news, so I must have been mistaken.

All the negative stuff I had heard and read about him lessened in importance because I'd been given the rare opportunity to get to know the real person. He smiled and gestured for me to sit on one of the sofas. He sat across from me. The sofas in the center of the room were large, but his long legs were much higher than mine. His pants leg rose slightly, and I hoped he didn't have white socks on.

I let my gaze flick down to check. He didn't.

I got the impression he had just been told I was stopping by. Not even for a photo op. It seemed like it needed to be more official. I doubted my visit had even made his daily schedule. The informality and comfort of the greeting made the entire experience feel like just a couple of old friends saying hello to each other.

If I had ever imagined my first meeting with President Reagan—which I had not—this was a complete juxtaposition to what I would have conjured, sending all prior expectations right out the window. With Mrs. Reagan scrutinizing the

Lunch with Holly

President's daily comings and goings, getting in to see him defied everything I knew about her.

The President started our conversation saying Colorado was one of the most beautiful states.

I said, "Yes, Mr. President, I agree."

He offered jelly beans. They were everywhere in his office. I declined.

The rest of the conversation was a blur until his words snapped me back to crystal-clear reality.

"I understand you want to work with me."

I agreed again. He said "with" him, not "for" him. That conjunction told me he saw his people as part of a team effort. The President walked me to the door.

In that three-minute moment, I was both inconsequential and awesome. It was, indeed, an extraordinary moment in an ordinary day.

An escort ushered me to a White House exit. I leaned against the bricks and closed my eyes to take it all in.

I still needed to learn what my job would be. A problem for another day. I walked back to the hotel, chin lifted a bit higher, steps a bit lighter, and called my parents—collect. A "collect" call allowed me to place a call at the called party's expense.

Mommy and Daddy answered at the same time. Mommy was, undoubtedly, upstairs; Daddy was downstairs watching a sports game with a cold one in hand.

He asked, "How's it going, Trudi Babe?"

I responded, "Fine, Daddy."

"Good to hear." Click. The usual conversation with Daddy - quick. He had to get back to the game and his beer.

"What's going on, Trudi?" Mommy sounded tired.

I asked her, "Are you alright, Mommy?"

She said, "I'm just winded from working in the garden. I'll send you pictures. The mint is ground cover. You know how it spreads like a weed. My petunias are thriving and the –"

I interrupted. I couldn't contain my excitement.

WINNING THE BATTLE AGAINST MYSELF

"I'm so sorry I interrupted you, but I just met with President Reagan."

"What?"

"It is unbelievable, isn't it?"

"George, pick up the phone," she shouted.

"What? I'm watching the game. What is it?"

"Pick up the phone!"

"I can't hear well on this phone. Can't you tell me about it later?"

"No. Trudi met with President Reagan!" she exclaimed.

"With who?"

"The President."

I almost nodded off amidst their back and forth. Daddy's voice brought me back.

"What happened, Trudi Babe?"

"I met with President Reagan in the Oval Office."

"Hot tamale knows!" This saying never made sense. What could a tamale possibly know?

Maybe he meant that a hot tamale had a nose. Either way, it was stupid.

"Tell us everything," Mommy was excited.

I conveyed the events to them step-by-step, to the intermittent questions. Their exhilaration choked me up. I stopped talking and listened to their laughter and felt their wonder, and pride.

"What happens next?" Daddy asked.

"I'm not sure. Maybe someone will call me.

***

Three days later, I received a call from the White House Office of Personnel regarding my job offer. My starting salary was going to be $55,000. Growing up, I thought I'd be successful if I made as much money annually as my age. That tells you I didn't grow up in a family that worshiped money because had I, I would have known how ludicrous that goal was.

Chapter 11

It's Black, It's White

> *"We all require and want respect, man or woman, black or white. It's our basic human right."*
>
> — Aretha Franklin

My White House tenure began in July 1983. My office was in the Old Executive Office Building. That's where the majority of staff offices were located. It was my third day at work, and I had yet to receive a White House pass for entry each day. I hadn't been put on the "access" list. I waited 25 minutes at the West Gate to get in each day. Luckily, although they changed every week, I established friendly relations with the West Gate guards, so they would laugh and joke with me while I awaited the clearance process.

My parents and I received numerous congratulatory messages regarding my appointment at the White House. One of the most notable cards was from Minoru Yasui on July 11, 1983. Min was the first Japanese American attorney admitted to the Oregon State Bar. He was one of the few Japanese Americans after the bombing of Pearl Harbor who fought laws that directly targeted Japanese Americans or Japanese immigrants. His case was the first to test the constitutionality of the curfews targeted at minority groups.

WINNING THE BATTLE AGAINST MYSELF

His case would go to the United States Supreme Court on June 21, 1943, where his conviction for breaking curfew was affirmed. After internment during most of World War II, he moved to Denver in 1944 and became a local leader in civic affairs, including leadership positions in the Japanese American Citizens League. In 1986, his criminal conviction was overturned by the Federal court. Min received a posthumous Presidential Medal of Freedom from President Barack Obama in a White House ceremony on November 24, 2015.

A letter of congratulations to my parents for my White House appointment on July 7, 1983, from an early mentor, Leonard Campbell, of Gorsuch, Kirgis, Campbell, Walker, and Grover, wrote that "in the original [article] and on the copies, justice is not done to Trudi's beauty which is comparable to her talent …" Of course, I'd include that comment in this book.

My first meeting was at 10:00 am with Jane Erkenbeck, an assistant to Nancy Reagan. I knew Jane from H.U.D., where she was Phil Winn's (Colorado Republican Party chair and Federal Housing Commissioner) secretary. Jane came to my office to help me find supplies and introduce me to the White House administrative support staff. She asked me to find out her salary if she became my secretary.

After a morning with the White House Interior Designer, insiders told me that the best way to get decent furniture was to retrieve it from an office of an employee who recently left. Otherwise, the furniture graveyard was the alternative.

Heeding their advice, another new employee, Mary Ann, Faith's press secretary, and I watched an office without an occupant for three weeks. We finally summoned the courage to take out selected pieces of furniture. My office decor was coming together nicely: one Victorian pearl gold sofa, two Victorian pearl ivory armchairs, two carved mahogany octagon end tables, and two antique brass candlestick lamps.

I covered my walls with framed posters of black women, including Fanny Lou Hamer, Wilma Rudolph, Ida B. Wells,

It's Black, It's White

Ella Jo Baker, Shirley Chisholm, Katherine Johnson, Mary McLeod Bethune, Claudette Colvin, Marian Wright Edelman, Madam C.J. Walker, Ruby Bridges, Lyda Newman, Mae Jemison, and others.

Then I received a call from the head of White House Security, George Sanders. He wanted to stop by for a visit. George was middle-aged, solidly built, with friendly eyes. I welcomed him and offered him water. He accepted and commented on my tasteful furniture.

I was proud of the compliment. He then explained the White House rules regarding furniture and politely informed me he would assist in returning the furniture to the proper owners. He said he knew of the furniture legend, but it needed to be more accurate. I was too humiliated to be embarrassed. George and I became good friends after that. He even helped me decorate my office with legitimate furniture far from my Victorian paradise.

The highlight of my first week at the White House was the reception and dinner I attended with Faith aboard the former presidential yacht, the U.S.S. Sequoia. I went to Faith's office at 5:20 pm. The two of us got into a car with telephones on each side of the backseat. The driver and dispatcher agreed the yacht was docked at Pier One in the Washington Navy Yard. It wasn't there. After several calls back and forth, the driver found the ship on the East Potomac Dock. We boarded at 6:10 pm and met with congressional leadership and a few state delegations. I drank champagne and stuffed my belly with hors d'oeuvres, all served on silver platters. The driver picked us up at 7:30 pm and took us to dinner at The George Town Club, where Faith had a membership.

The George Town Club was an 18th-century row house on Wisconsin Avenue, the main street in Georgetown. Membership was by invitation only, and all prospective members had to contact their primary sponsor. You had to know somebody that knew somebody that knew somebody else and on and on ... The restaurant was stunning with fishing vessel figureheads framing a leaded glass demi-lune window. My meal was a lump crab cake, house salad, grilled salmon, sauteed spinach and mushrooms, and a light, fluffy chocolate mousse. The driver picked us up at 9:30 pm. I was home in bed by 10:20 pm.

Getting a secretary was like pulling teeth. I was disregarded at every turn by these Republicans. Perhaps the hope was that I would only do something if I had some help. As it was, my office was on the fourth floor of the Old Executive Office Building, and all but two other professional staffers, Mary Ann and Linus, had offices on the first floor. My office location made it easier for me to be out of sight, out of mind. My office was the size of three offices on the first floor.

The most generous interpretation of office placement would be that Mary Ann and I were the newest employees, and no open offices remained on the first floor. In all candor, there probably weren't any offices on the first floor, but had there been, I doubt I would have been offered one.

These Republicans were paradoxical psychos. They wanted me to go and stay at the same time. They were what the songwriter Kris Kristofferson would have called "a walking contradiction" from The Pilgrim: Chapter 33 from his 1972 album *The Silver-Tongued Devil and I*. I was in my third week without a secretary when I headed to Faith's office.

"We have a problem, Faith. Why can't I get a secretary?"

She lied to my face, "You don't have a secretary?"

"I won't waste any more time talking to you. I'm sure the press would love to hear that I can't get a secretary. And the President would undoubtedly promote you once this hits the papers," I said sarcastically. I got a secretary that afternoon.

My secretary's first words were, "You are such a credit to your race."

Here we go—. To my shame, I let it ride. I allowed my need for a secretary to outweigh my desire to draw blood from this woman's nose.

It's Black, It's White

I attended a luncheon with Republican women officials on January 13, 1984, in the White House State Dining Room. I located my seat and admired the hand-drawn calligraphy place cards. The menu paired Chardonnay with a salad of bay scallops & lobster, tenderloin of veal in Chablis, and soft-shell pasta Florentine. The meal concluded with fresh berries in tender pastry shells.

Servers carried the wine with white hand towels draped over their forearms. I didn't want any wine. I'm not too fond of Chardonnay. When you feel out of place, have no conversation, and no one is interested in bringing you into their discussion, drinking wine becomes your only option, whether you like it or not.

The President and Mrs. Reagan came in, and we all stood up and applauded. I sipped my way through glass number one.

I signaled a waiter, "May I have another white wine?"

He poured, and I drank. I should have asked for champagne. I love good champagne. Sometimes, champagne is the only thing to get a girl through.

As Coco Chanel noted, "I only drink Champagne on two occasions, when I am in love and when I am not."

Twenty minutes after their arrival, President Reagan tapped his glass, stood, and went to the podium as I asked for a third glass of wine. I was feeling queasy from the wine I hated.

The President welcomed the audience and said, "[A]nd I hope that you're all as happy as I am that we have with us two of the most important women in my life — Nancy and Maureen... And I must mention Trudi Morrison, who runs a program close to my heart — the 50 States Project."

The President signaled me to stand. I was stunned, nervous, and slightly drunk.

Maureen, the President's daughter, must have put my name in his speech. She had suddenly and suspiciously taken great interest in me. I have a photo with President Reagan where he recognized me and called me by name in a reception line.

WINNING THE BATTLE AGAINST MYSELF

The photo of that reception line shows Maureen is behind me in the picture. The reception was immediately before the luncheon with Republican women officials. Apparently, President Reagan didn't remember who I was, even though my contact with him and my name were mentioned in his imminent luncheon speech.

Figure 20. -President Reagan and Trudi, 1983.

Maureen and her father must have worked out an arrangement whereby he would know who I was because I was in line in front of Maureen. That was the signal. Because why would Maureen stand in line to greet her father? Seeing her would make it appear that the President knew me. It took years for me to figure out this scheme.

The audience applauded, and I often wondered if the response was because I was black. The audience went overboard to make me feel accepted, or was it because the audience supported the Project and knew that I was taking hits delivering the President's message, or was it both? I suspected the audience thought I was the black female sacrificial fool taking the crap from those who hated me and the President's policies.

It's Black, It's White

The most memorable thing from that White House luncheon was meeting Associate Justice of the United States Supreme Court, Sandra Day O'Connor. President Reagan nominated Sandra Day O'Connor to the Supreme Court on August 19, 1981, making her the first woman on the highest court in the United States since its creation in 1789. Justice O'Connor approached me, commending my efforts to weed out disparities against women. Her words humbled me.

The following day, Nancy Reagan was on television defending herself over something. I was late leaving home, so I missed the story. I viewed Nancy Reagan as self-possessed and distant. She didn't look at me; she looked through me as if I didn't exist or were an inanimate object. I found Mrs. Reagan very guarded, smug, self-serving, and self-righteous. I must have been too low on the food chain for her to bother with.

Nothing was more symbolic of Mrs. Reagan's refinement than her wardrobe born of its designers. To my surprise, at one of the 1984 Inaugural Balls (there were 7 or 8 Inaugural Balls), Mrs. Reagan, always the epitome of elegance, acknowledged my presence with an impersonal nod and disapproving glance at my meager cleavage, which was exaggerated by the designer gown I wore.

I shared my "cleavage" moment with Holly Coors. She tilted her head back, laughing so hard I could see her fillings.

She said, "Well, Trudi, if you got it — flaunt it!"

Mrs. Reagan was a fierce protector of her husband. She had incredible political judgment and was heavily involved in White House personnel matters. Trust, however, was not Mrs. Reagan's default position. Toward the end of my White House tenure, after James Baker, Reagan's chief of staff, and Donald Regan, Treasury Secretary, swapped jobs, I observed Mrs. Reagan's seminal role in setting the stage for ridding Regan of her husband's White House.

After Regan's arrival at the White House, his hubris overwhelmed him, forcing him to go to the front of the line and repeat each name he had heard. Somehow, his perfect replication failed when he got to me. He called me Zelda. Who was Zelda? Was there someone in his life named Zelda? What was going on? He hadn't messed up any other names. His memory game was impressive until he got to me. Hmm ... How was I different from everyone else? Let's guess. This boded badly for my job longevity.

Regan wanted to avoid Mrs. Reagan's involvement in personnel decisions. Michael Deaver, a long-time friend of the Reagans, was Nancy Reagan's tool for getting things done without her fingerprints. An example was her sharing Joan Quigley's, an astrologer, guidance with Regan for scheduling purposes and Regan's rumors about the perceived chaos it caused. In his 1988 "tell-all" book, Regan lambasted her after being ousted from the White House in 1987. He disclosed that Mrs. Reagan used astrology to decide the timing of presidential speeches and trips.

"Virtually every move and decision the Reagans made during my time as the White House chief of staff was cleared in advance by a woman in San Francisco who drew up horoscopes to make certain that the planets were in a favorable alignment for the enterprise," Regan wrote.

Regan's backstabbing was undercurrent gossip at the White House and even filtered down to my level. Regan should have kept his mouth shut. Michael Deaver was the one who alerted Mrs. Reagan to the Regan betrayal. I had left the job by then, but remaining allies told me that the straw that broke Regan's back was the 1987 disclosure that the President had secretly approved arms sales to Iran. Mrs. Reagan blamed Regan for not protecting her husband and her blame was correctly placed because of Regan's tactics.

Mrs. Reagan, although she would never admit it, was a feminist when feminism was changing positions of power. Her power came from creating the President's agenda based on her convictions, which she stuck to. She took on issues of importance to women, such as embryonic stem cell research and the AIDS crisis thanks to the prodding of Dionne Warwick. A different viewpoint was expressed by Gloria Steinem, leader and spokeswoman for the American feminist movement in the late 1960s and early 1970s and a co-founder of Ms. Magazine. In a Ms. Magazine article, she described Mrs. Reagan as "the rare woman who can perform the miracle of having no interests at all."

But, in all fairness, Mrs. Reagan did enjoy a decadent display of wealth. During my tenure, she was dubbed the porcelain princess because of the china pattern debacle. As shocking as it was to learn that Mrs. Reagan spent $209,508 on dishes, the dismay was compounded by the President naming ketchup a vegetable the same day. Equally, what made no sense was how she hated governmental handouts but enjoyed paying wholesale or getting her designer wardrobe free. Keeping with Reagan's campaign promises to pull the American people out of hard times, his first inauguration turned out to be a luxurious display of opulence, including furs, jewels, limousines, gowns, and custom tuxedos. Later criticisms of the cost of the festivities—an estimated 16 million dollars—caused the President to tone down the celebration considerably the second time around. How could the President and First Lady, who grew up poor, forget that fact? In Washington, people were unemployed, hungry, and homeless, a stone's throw from the White House.

I started an informal group of black women appointees named Black Republican Women's Network. The idea was to share ideas and opportunities. I conducted briefings in the Indian Treaty Room in the East Wing of the Old Executive Office Building.

"When I came back to Washington, [Trudi] called me for no other reason other than I was here and was another black woman," said Antoinette Ford, an assistant administrator at the Agency for International Development.

"[Trudi] helped those of us in the administration help one another, whether it was an issue we were working on, such as child support enforcement, or different employment opportunities, said Stephanie Lee Miller, assistant secretary for public affairs at H.H.S."

Some of my invitations to briefings were signed 'Yours in Sisterhood.' The group didn't go far; a couple of luncheons and meetings. People were too busy or afraid to participate because of race-based loathing. Those who feared because of race didn't want to be associated with a group of other blacks. Frequent depictions of ourselves fuel race self-hatred as drug dealers, prostitutes, lazy, less intelligent, dishonest, shiftless, and retrograde images. Perhaps some group members recognized those in the Administration who didn't want blacks to have more power.

Editor-in-Chief of Essence Magazine, Susan Taylor, called me in early January 1985. She told me I was nominated as the first Essence Woman. I knew that Essence prided itself on speaking "directly to a black woman's spirit, heart, and unique concerns." Ms. Taylor explained that the Essence Woman was a new magazine section designed to highlight black women who have moved their lives forward personally, professionally, intellectually, and spiritually, and urge other black women do the same. I was overwhelmed and humbled.

Ms. Taylor was soft-spoken and gracious. We talked about our lives and the challenges we still faced. A few days later, I got another call from Essence Magazine. The call was from Eric Copage. He informed me I was selected as the first Essence Woman for the March 1985 issue, page 54.

At its apex were seven blacks in the Reagan White House: Wendell Wilkie Gunn, Steven Rhodes, Fred McClure, Mel Bradley, George Armstrong, John Tiller, William Keyes, and me. I was the highest-ranked black woman in the White House. But how high was the highest? A couple of female Special Assistants, Deputy Assistants, and Faith, the only female Assistant out of eighteen, were ranked above me. Even with my low rank and six women outranking me, I had to claim my place. Three blacks left between the November 1984 election and a few months after the January 1985 inauguration.

Chapter 12

Merrymaking

"There's a scripture that says, 'A merry heart doeth good like medicine.' I think that's true, too."

-Dolly Parton

During my tenure, there were some high points: inaugural balls with designer gowns, seats in the presidential box at the Kennedy Center and Ford Theater, press conferences, and representing the President at numerous events. Lionel Hampton came to a White House dinner and told me he had worked with my grandfather. What a mind-blower! Lionel Hampton was a jazz musician and bandleader, known as a skilled drummer, pianist, and singer, and showmanship as a performer. He achieved his biggest recorded hit, Flying Home, with the tenor saxophone solo by Illinois Jacquet, Mommy's cousin.

I had a fun day at work when friends Meadowlark Lemon, Rosie Grier, and Ernie Banks visited. They were good athletes. I had met them years before at a social event. Meadowlark was a basketball player with the Harlem Globetrotters. He was the "Clown Prince" of the Globetrotters and was enshrined in the Naismith Memorial Basketball Hall of Fame in 2003. Rosie was a football player and a cousin of my sister's good friend, Pam Grier, best known for portraying tough and sexy crime

WINNING THE BATTLE AGAINST MYSELF

fighters in 1970s films. We grew up with Pam and her brother Rodney, an excellent artist. Ernie was a baseball player. He was inducted into the National Baseball Hall of Fame in 1977 and was named to the Major League Baseball All-Century Team in 1999. I took them to meet President Reagan and lunch in the White House Mess. They argued about the most challenging sports during lunch: basketball, football, or baseball.

Things started getting loud. Meadowlark finally asked me to settle the dispute. I regaled them with stories of my lack of athletic prowess, and we laughed so loud that we decided they'd better get their dessert "to go." We spent the rest of the day telling each other lies in my office. It was a grand day. Later that same year, Rosie was booked on television shows to talk about being a born-again Christian and a featured speaker at the 1984 Republican National Convention. On August 20, 1984, he endorsed President Reagan for re-election during its evening session.

Michael Jackson, the King of Pop, came to the White House on May 14, 1984, to receive The Presidential Public Safety Commendation for his song, Beat It. Michael allowed Reagan to use the song for Nancy Reagan's anti-drunk driving campaign. In his speech, President Reagan said that some of Michael's fans "said to tell Michael, 'Please give some T.L.C. to the P.Y.T.s.' I know that sounds a little 'off the wall,' but we know what I mean. Michael, I have another message from your fans in the Washington, D.C., area. They said, 'We want you back.' So, when you begin your greatly awaited cross-country tour, please drop off here in the nation's capital."

I was surprised at the extent of Michael's shyness. He whispered "Hi" to me and put his head down. I said, "Bless you, Michael." He blushed again. Michael barely said two words before and after the presentation in the holding room. He was so nervous before walking outside with the President. He went to the bathroom twice within 2-4 minutes.

Merrymaking

In June 1984, Jet Magazine sponsored a survey to determine the most responsive black Republican in the Reagan Administration.

On June 21, 1984, Dr. Ralph David Abernathy, Dr. Martin Luther King Jr.'s chief aide, wrote, *"I take this opportunity to nominate Ms. Trudi Morrison, the Associate Director of the White House Office of Public Liaison. Ms. Morrison is keenly aware of the delicate balance between the execution of public policy and serving the particular needs and demands of a black constituency. I have found Ms. Morrison to be most responsive to requests and inquiries, even when the needs are beyond the parameters and scope of her immediate office. She is approachable and consistently demonstrates a commendable peripatetic professional style that provides an open-door policy for black Americans seeking the assistance of the highest office in the land."*

I came in first in the survey, becoming the most responsive black in the Reagan Administration.

I wondered if this was a high point, but I thought the outcome was superb. This was when I received the call from Senator Lawton Chiles (R-FL) regarding the New Testament reading at The National Prayer Breakfast in February 1986.

The next day, Senator Chiles came to my office to ask if I was married because my husband and I had different last names. I assured him I was, but he still asked me to bring my marriage license to work the next day. I thought it was more important to deliver the word of God than to start an uproar because of one man's ignorance.

Senator Mark Hatfield of Oregon introduced the President. Among those participating in the breakfast program were Jacob Javits, a former U.S. Senator from New York, and Barbara Jordan, a former U.S. Representative from Texas.

Senator Chiles said, "Please let me present Trudi Michelle Morrison, another one of those who faithfully serve the Senate, with a reading from the New Testament." I read from Matthew,

WINNING THE BATTLE AGAINST MYSELF

Chapter 6, verses 25 through 34, and Matthew, Chapter 7, verses 7 through 12.

When Brad Reynolds, Assistant Attorney General for Civil Rights (Justice Department), opposed a policy guaranteeing a percentage of federal contracts to minority businesses in Dade County, Florida, I wrote a memo advising the President against Brad's approach.

I had no idea what he was going to do. After all, Brad said in my presence, "Discrimination based on race is illegal, immoral, unconstitutional, inherently wrong, and destructive of a democratic society."

On March 30, 1981, fewer than 100 days into his presidency, President Reagan was shot in the chest. The President had just finished addressing a labor meeting at the Washington Hilton Hotel. He was walking with his entourage to his limousine when six shots were fired at him, hitting Reagan and three of his attendants. The White House press secretary James Brady was shot in the head and critically wounded, Secret Service agent Timothy McCarthy was shot in the side, and District of Columbia policeman Thomas Delahanty was shot in the neck. Larry Speaks became acting press secretary because Jim Brady suffered permanent brain damage. A month later, I received a call from Larry Speakes, acting press secretary, since Jim Brady was still in the hospital after the assassination attempt.

Larry Speaks said the President wanted me to accompany him to a forum in the afternoon.

Riding in the Presidential motorcade with the Secret Service hanging on the sides of the moving limousine was exhilarating. Bulletproof glass panels separated the seat rows.

I didn't know where we were going, but I was sure they wouldn't kidnap a black woman White House aide. I had no money, no fame, and no children. Plus, the press would be relentless. Nonetheless, I kept in mind that these men in stately uniforms had a good cover, the President's limo. Black folks

Merrymaking

have been kidnapped, raped, and lynched for less. At least my parents would have been proud that I was dressed nicely.

We entered the Washington Hilton, where I walked next to President Reagan. He told me to stand at the backstage curtain. The Secret Service already had their orders based on the President's instructions and showed me exactly where to stand.

The President walked to the on-stage microphone to huge applause. He started a speech to the National Association of Minority Contractors where he said that "such 'set-asides' were consistent with his Federal policy. And he intended to keep it that way."

He turned and smiled at me. Wow ... Magic, I had an impact and made a difference. Often, my job was not to make something happen but to prevent something from happening. Now, I had diverted the course of the river.

Chapter 13

Otherness

"...You may trod me in the very dirt
But still, like dust, I'll rise."

-Maya Angelou
(Still, I Rise)

In 1984, I wrote a reference letter on White House stationery for an associate referred by a close friend. As I recall, this was about a promotion: the man was already on the National Endowment for the Humanities staff, chaired by William Bennett, but felt Bennett was biased against him because he was black. I discounted that notion because I didn't know Bennett. Bennett complained to the White House about my letter using White House stationery, resulting in a disciplinary call. That same year, Bennett crafted the "p.c." debates.

In *To Reform A Legacy: A Report on the Humanities in Higher Education*, Bennett argued that curriculum reformers in higher education were denying students a timeless legacy by replacing "classic texts" of Western civilization with works of lesser quality and significance. He posits that 60s reformers, now university professors, threaten a precious American heritage by favoring a more inclusive curriculum. Hmm ... precisely what people would comprise "a more inclusive curriculum?" Let's guess.

Otherness

And here's the topper: Bennett was Secretary of Education from 1985-1987 under Reagan.

In his first public speech after becoming Secretary of Education, Bennett said, "In my view, there are still too many schools in which our students are taught that this country's past is primarily a history of racism, pollution, oppression, and inequality." And he finds this erroneous; how, in what regard?

On a voter registration swing through the South, I praised the Republican record and urged that more Republican politicians hire blacks for jobs. In Mississippi, I was asked what Senator Thad Cochran, in a tight race, needed to do to attract black voters. I replied that a good start would be hiring blacks on his staff. Thus began the firestorm. State Grand Ole Party (GOP) officials circulated letters asking that I be muzzled or removed. The first call was from a friend, Frank Donatelli, Faith's Deputy. He demanded I issue an immediate retraction.

Next was a call from Thelma Duggin, another friend at the Republican National Committee, informing me I was wrong: Senator Cochran had blacks on his staff. I vaguely recall speaking to Jim Cicconi, an ally, and James A. Baker III (Reagan's Chief of Staff) assistant, with a similar message. I clarified my statement to the press: "The White House told me to retract my statement."

A few days after I returned to the White House, Faith called me in the morning and told me to write a letter of apology to Senator Cochran. That same afternoon, she told me to meet her at the carpool. I didn't have a chance to ask where we were going.

We rode in silence to the Senate Hart Building. I walked with her as we entered Thad Cochran's office. I was so glad I hadn't written a letter of apology. The appointment had been scheduled ahead of time. Faith approached the receptionist and said that I had a meeting with Cochran. Me? I didn't make an appointment. I was so through with Faith. We sat together in silence for at least 45 minutes.

Cochran's chief of staff said, "Faith, the Senator is on the floor. He didn't know you were coming." Cochran planned to make me come to him and then not show up. He planned to snub me, put me in my place, and set this uppity woman straight. Faith and I left and rode back to the White House in silence. I never heard another word about it.

I was Elaine Jenkins' protégé. Howard Jenkins, Elaine's husband, was a law professor and became the first black to be appointed to the U.S. National Labor Relations Board (NLRB) when nominated by President John F. Kennedy. He was reappointed by three subsequent presidents and served on the NLRB for 20 years. Elaine repeatedly urged me to run for office. Despite their busy days, Elaine and Howard managed to get home for their 6:30 p.m. martini together daily.

Feeling like "the other" among Republicans was a fact of existence in the White House — and in the Party itself. I was "the other" on many apparent levels. I gave speeches nationwide, including my belief that black people and women needed a voice and platform in both major political parties. Believing is one thing; acting on that belief is another.

I hadn't planned to go to the 1984 GOP Convention in Dallas, Texas, but Elaine convinced me that my presence was imperative as the only black woman in the White House. Women supporting women and blacks backing blacks was my purpose.

Chapter 14

Smooth Landing

"The personal things should be left out of platforms at conventions. You can argue yourself blue in the face, and you're not going to change each other's minds. It's a waste of your time and my time."

-**Barbara Bush**

I arrived near sunset in Dallas for the National Republican Convention at 5:46 pm. on American Airlines Flight 163 on Saturday, August 18, 1984. I witnessed the bright sky with baby blues and light pinks. Someone planned for transportation because a man with a cardboard sign with my name on it was in the baggage claim area. I asked for his identification as he grabbed my bags from the carousel.

"Who sent you to pick me up?" I paid for the entire trip, so I certainly wouldn't have rented a limousine.

"I don't know. My dispatcher handles all that."

I followed him to his limousine and got in. The driver took me to the Downtown Sheraton on North Olive Street off North Dallas Parkway. The driver was chatty. He talked about the expense to taxpayers by staging a national convention in Dallas and spoke of Republicans with contempt for overrunning his city.

WINNING THE BATTLE AGAINST MYSELF

He expressed the view, with absolute confidence, that I was not a Republican because I was black. I decided not to respond and save my strength for the upcoming week of battling Republican bias. I was already preparing myself for imminent settings in which black people were typically absent, not expected, and marginalized when present. Some white folks don't get it. They don't understand or acknowledge the minute-by-minute stresses black people live with because of skin color. Understanding racism and race-related stress were pervasive.

Whenever my black son left the house, I worried about him making it home safely because of police brutality. I dealt with racism while shopping (being followed through the store), driving ("profiling" black drivers), exercising (safety concerns as a barrier to outdoor activity in white neighborhoods–particularly those of higher socioeconomic status, for reasons related to violence, lack of sidewalks, and even unleashed dogs), and walking (young white men in the bed of the truck driving by flying a confederate flag and yelling obscenities at me).

Race, stereotypes, prejudice, and condescension flourished regarding "otherness," the way people devalue dissimilar others. Race is a social construct based on beliefs that all members of the same race share given characteristics.

"I am a Republican," I said to the cab driver. "Here's a major problem: most people don't stop to consider when views like opposition to, for example, busing or affirmative action would not be racist. Some of these views are not racist on their face. But, conceding that these views could, in theory, be non-racist, many insist they are never non-racist in practice. Opposition to busing or affirmative action is not equivalent to discrimination. Carrying out that resistance in a discriminatory way is equivalent to racism. Unfortunately, both sides shut down at this point, and the conversation ends."

"I didn't think of it like that. Good luck this week," the driver said. I got out of the cab.

Smooth Landing

I was at the Convention as a reminder that we existed and that our community had policy preferences that should be included in the platform. Those preferences included access to quality health care, housing, jobs, education, police, criminal justice reform, equal pay for black women, and voting rights. I was alone, with no position of power. I spoke to three people on the platform committee. None of the concerns I discussed were included in the final document. I wondered if those three people brought those issues forth. Republicans will not and should not win black voters through racial sleight of hand.

After checking into the hotel, I walked to the Arena Center in the Convention Hall to pick up my credentials.

"Hey, Judi." Judi Buckalew and I worked together in the Office of Public Liaison. She was a blonde with a beautiful face and a gentle manner.

"Trudi! when did you get in?"

"About an hour ago. Is Cathi here yet?" Cathi Villalpando and Judi are my best friends in the White House. Judi and I attempted to work out at a nearby gym, and Cathi became the second Hispanic Treasurer of the United States. Cathi was, in large part, responsible for my becoming Deputy Sergeant at Arms of the Senate. She was a stunning woman who wore exquisite clothes every day.

"I don't think she's gotten in yet."

"Let's go to the LTV reception at Union Station. We can get free food there."

"Cool. Let's go."

Taxis were lined up outside the hotel. We were dropped off at Union Station and followed the signs to the Studebaker Club, where we ate.

Sunday morning, August 19, started with a Prayer Breakfast in the Reunion Ballroom C at the Hyatt. After breakfast, I returned to the hotel and slept for a few hours. At 4:00, I attended a "Women in Government" press party at the Convention Center. I looked around the room and spotted

WINNING THE BATTLE AGAINST MYSELF

Judi and Cathi. They came over and hugged me.

"What kind of food do they have over there?" Judi asked, pointing to one of the buffet tables.

"We shouldn't eat here, Judi. The barbecue is tonight, remember? Cathi said.

"That's right. I forgot. What are you guys wearing?"

"I packed a pantsuit," I said.

"So did I," Cathi said. Knowing Cathi, her pantsuit was made-to-order by an expensive designer. Everything she wore was custom-tailored and gorgeous.

"Let's meet in the hotel lobby at 5:15 so we can ride the bus together for the reception and dinner," Judi said.

"Sounds good. See you guys then," I said.

We go our separate ways, combing the room as the White House folks know to do.

The three of us were prompt and boarded the bus at 5:20. The bus stopped at H.L. Hunt's Estate for a reception. H.L. Hunt was a gambler-turned-oil-prospector who built a financial empire from a small early investment. In his later years, he was perhaps the world's richest man and became a Republican powerhouse.

After the reception, Cathi and Judi went to other events. I was invited to Southfork Ranch for a barbeque. Southfork was a fictional name in a 1978 television show named Dallas. The real property was designated Mount Vernon, a magnificent white-pillared colonial mansion with undulating shrubs bordering a sweeping, manicured lawn that trailed off the water.

The Dallas television show character, J.R. Ewing, was based on Ray Lee Hunt, the Dallas billionaire oilman. H.L. Hunt was Ray Lee Hunt's father.

Alberta Hunter, a jazz and blues singer, provided entertainment. Seeing her slapped me back to my "otherness" status. She, Secretary Pierce, and I were the only blacks there. Ms. Hunter died two months later, on October 17, 1984, at age 89.

At the barbeque, there was a whole pig on a rotisserie. I swear its eyes followed me as it went round and round on the

Smooth Landing

rotisserie spit. I was squeamish about the squishy eyes. There was an apple in its mouth. I nearly fainted when a guy pulled the meat off the pig with his hands, slopped it on a plate, and handed me the plate. This was too much for me.

A buffet table had fried chicken, beef brisket, macaroni salad, potato salad, cornbread, rolls, apple sauce, sugar peas, glazed carrots, corn on the cob, baked beans, and alcoholic and non-alcoholic drinks. Despite the cornucopia of food, the table wobbled. The dessert table had fresh fruit, cookies, cake, carved watermelons, pies, and ice cream. The buffet table was deliciously imperfect.

I decided to stroll through the ranch grounds. There was a barn with the stinky smell of animal waste. Pew! The combination of manure and feed spoilage made me gag. Holding my breath, I made an immediate right turn and smelled the sweet odor of alfalfa hay—what a contrast to the frivolity of the barbeque. The roasted pig, the barn stench, and the sweetness of the grass made me lightheaded. I stumbled to the bus and stretched out on the long seat in the back. I slept until someone woke me up when we returned to the hotel. I went to my room and fell asleep in my clothes.

The National Federation of Republican Women honored Republican women leaders at a 7:30 breakfast Monday morning at Union Station. The organization prides itself on empowering women in the political process and giving women a platform to serve as leaders in the political, government, and civic arenas. I was hesitant about leaving the comfortable ambiance I enjoyed in the hotel. I pulled the covers over my head and went back to sleep.

The 6:00 pm. hour was Lamar Hunt's Ball. Lamar was the son of oil tycoon H. L. Hunt. Cathi, Judi, and I planned to meet in the hotel lobby at 5:30. We knew plenty of food would be at the ball.

I dressed in my full-length black sequined gown. I was stunning. I put on my rhinestone necklace and diamond earrings.

WINNING THE BATTLE AGAINST MYSELF

My black patent 3-inch heels were perfect with the dress, even though I couldn't walk far in them. I was a sensation riding down the escalator.

People pointed, men smiled, and women politely glanced. The attention drew Judi and Cathi's attention.

"Wow," Judi said loudly; Cathi grinned from ear to ear. Mary Jo, our White House colleague, was standing with them.

"That's what I call an entrance," Mary Jo said. Mary Jo was highly connected in the business world. She had a cute, round face and wore her hair in a bob with bangs.

"You look chic," Cathi said.

"Thanks. You guys clean up well, too," I said.

"I have a limo waiting. Wanna ride?" Mary Jo asked.

We piled into the limo and headed to Former President Gerald Ford's keynote address. The former President seemed very decent with great humility. He represented civility in politics. President Ford had a victory amid defeat. He healed our land but was the only unelected President because of President Nixon's resignation. I fell asleep during his boring speech.

Wednesday's events began with the First Lady's Luncheon at Loews Anatole Hotel's Chantilly Ballroom. The luncheon and Mrs. Reagan's appearance couldn't have been more uneventful. The day's exception was the afternoon keynote address.

Jeane Kirkpatrick gave a memorable keynote address at that afternoon's 1984 GOP Convention as the first woman to serve as Ambassador to the United Nations. Kirkpatrick delivered a blistering speech dealing exclusively with foreign policy. Kirkpatrick's delivery was measured and timely.

Even though she kept her language clear, her topic, "They Always Blame America First," was complex, and few convention attendees knew what she was talking about. A measured delivery aided her in putting her points across and keeping the crowd with her.

The evening dinner was hosted by E.F. Hutton, a significant securities brokerage and investment banking firm emphasizing retail service for individual investors. The nomination of presidential and vice-presidential candidates followed dinner.

Figure 21. -1st Woman UN Ambassador Jeane Kirkpatrick & Faith Ryan Whittlesey Ambassador to Switzerland March, 1985.jpg.

Conventions finalize a party's choice for presidential and vice-presidential nominees. The delegates choose the nominees, most bound by primary votes.

To become the presidential nominee, a candidate typically has to win a majority of delegates. This usually happens through the party's primaries and caucuses. It's then confirmed through a vote of the delegates at the National Convention. Delegates at the National Convention are the only ones to cast a binding vote for the party nominee.

That exercise went on past midnight. Knowing the inevitable outcome, Reagan and Bush again, I walked to my hotel, showered, and went to bed.

Thursday, August 23, 1984, was the last day of the Republican National Convention. I slept in and visited hospitality suites and buffet tables. The evening brought the presidential and vice-presidential acceptance speeches.

Chapter 15

Equality or Not?

> *"The emotional, sexual, and psychological stereotyping of females begins when the doctor says: It's a girl."*
> -Shirley Chisholm

My title was Associate Director, Office of Public Liaison and Director of President Reagan's 50 States Initiative. The 50 States Initiative reflected President Reagan's campaign commitment with the 50 governors to identify and correct discriminatory state laws. My friend Thelma Duggin laid the groundwork for the program in May 1981 with a Presidential letter to the governors seeking assistance in identifying and correcting discriminatory state laws. In October 1981, the governor's representatives met at the White House to exchange information and promote cooperation between the states.

At a Republican luncheon in 1983, where women were dressed in their finery, a woman stood up and threw a tomato at me. She didn't like my speech supporting the 50 States Initiative instead of the Equal Rights Amendment (ERA)—the ERA aimed at inscribing gender equality in the Constitution. I was so glad I was wearing a red suit.

The police were called. They asked if I wanted the woman arrested, and I said yes. At the end of my speech, the police

Equality or Not?

asked me to press charges. I declined. I didn't want the woman to suffer; maybe it would be more instructive to learn that you don't attack the messenger bringing news of a policy you disagree with. Perhaps she would learn to be more open-minded.

I thought forgiveness was the way to go. The police released her. The woman wrote me a letter of regret and apology. The letter included, "As a woman, I know what you go through as a black woman." Until that sentence, I believed the episode was solely about policy. But no. It's always about race. In essence, she said my racial oppression is no different from her gender oppression, so she can't be racist or sexist. I saw another dichotomy: would she have felt comfortable throwing a projectile at a white woman representing policies she didn't like? Maybe. Maybe not.

My job entailed traveling to 50 states (I got to 38) and meeting with governors to identify and review regulations and statutes that disparately impacted gender. Changes to laws in every state were laborious work—searching through millions of documents—requiring expungement of the exclusionary language. I reviewed gender disparities in divorce, property, insurance, employment, etc.

Laws created by agencies were regulations; statutes authorized regulations. Regulations were subordinate to statutes. If the 50 States Initiative had been universally implemented, it would have been more effective than a Constitutional Amendment. There was no way three-quarters of the states would ratify a Constitutional Amendment, let alone a controversial one. It might have been possible to get many states to sign onto an Initiative to affirmatively make the things happen that the ERA was supposed to attain on the ground.

Phyllis Schlafly, head of the Eagle Forum, contacted me and invited me to dinner at her home. The Eagle Forum strongly opposed the ERA, and Phyllis had a moral ferocity about her. She had a tasteful home. The Eagle Forum ladies were gracious. They didn't discuss the 50 States Project or the ERA.

WINNING THE BATTLE AGAINST MYSELF

The Eagle Forum ladies wanted me to put faces with names of those who supported the President's Project. I surmised that Maureen Reagan was strategically befriending me to watch the Initiative's progress. She suggested that she and I co-host women's briefings at the White House. February 6, 1984, a Jet magazine article on page 13 informs that "Trudi Michelle Morrison, the highest-ranked woman at the White House, and Maureen Reagan, the President's daughter, co-chair the series of four day-long briefings for GOP women officeholders across the country. Participants in the White House briefings, which will end in March, include HUD Secretary Samuel Pierce [the only black Reagan cabinet member]."

Maureen was a staunch supporter of the ERA. If I were doing a poor job, Maureen would have had more sway with her father to support the ERA. I believe Maureen would have done anything to get her father's attention. Slight hints made me think that her stepmother, Nancy Reagan, blocked her access to her father.

Aside from possible motives, Maureen and I became friends and had many lunches and dinners. Her husband, Dennis Revell, was a down-to-earth good guy who was always glad to see me. Maureen and Dennis were generous, loving people. They had one daughter, Margaret "Rita" Mirembe Revell, who was orphaned in Uganda. They became Rita's guardians in 1994. They adopted her in 2001. It was a devastating blow when Maureen passed from skin cancer on August 8, 2001, at age 60.

When I put all my meetings with governors together, even though the Initiative would have been more thorough and effective on the ground immediately, the Democratic governors told me they feared an Initiative could be minimized or eradicated in the long run. Still, a Constitutional Amendment would be lasting equality for the genders. They needed more faith in the political process to support an Initiative. Initiatives can be undone. They wanted the Project enshrined in law, whether

Equality or Not?

case law or statute. Some of the other Democratic governors I met with included Jim Hunt (North Carolina), Jay Rockefeller (West Virginia), Chuck Robb (Virginia), Bruce King (New Mexico), Jim Folson (Alabama), and Roy Romer (Colorado).

The Republican governors were skeptical but supported the Project because it was Reagan's. I was repeatedly asked why we needed another vehicle to protect women. Isn't that what the 1963 Equal Pay Act was for? I often replied that the 1963 Equal Pay Act protects women and men against wage discrimination based on sex.

The Stop ERA movement had gained momentum and reached new constituencies in Southern battleground states, tapping into evangelical churches. Some of the Republican governors I met with included: Dick Thornburgh (Pennsylvania), Kit Bond (Missouri), John Sununu (New Hampshire), Pete du Pont (Delaware), Fife Symington (Arizona), Lawton Chiles (Florida), and Terry Branstad (Iowa).

Middle-of-the-road Democrat and Republican governors worried that the laws written to protect women — guaranteeing alimony and exempting women from combat — would be scrapped. A few of those with that view included John Engler (R-Michigan), Ben Nelson (D-Nebraska), George Voinovich (R-Ohio), Bruce Sundlun (D-Rhode Island), and Tommy Thompson (R-Wisconsin).

I was never convinced that the White House was aware or interested in the magnitude of the 50 States Project or what it could become. Did they even know there was a 50 States Project? Did the President know what the Project was when he mentioned my name? Probably not. Just because the President mentioned my name and said the Project was close to his heart didn't mean he really knew what the Project was about or even cared. At least someone had the political sense to tell the President that when he criticized the ERA, he should say that this did not mean he did not believe in gender equality. Politics isn't required to be honest or knowledgeable.

WINNING THE BATTLE AGAINST MYSELF

Successful politics needs someone to think that you believe what you're saying. If the White House had been aware or understood the power of this Initiative, they certainly wouldn't have put me in charge of the entire Project. A black woman directing a conservative President's Project for women during an election year when he's under fire for a "gender gap?" Come back to Earth, people! This is reality. Recall the comment in the Washington Post about me being viewed as "window dressing."

At the time, the Democratic Party asked Democratic governors to snub the White House requests for information on differences in state laws that discriminate based on sex. With public opinion polls showing Reagan's popularity among women voters substantially less than among men, a "gender gap" developed, and both parties wanted to appeal to women.

I sent letters and questionnaires to all 50 governors in March 1984, asking them to list recent changes in state legislation and regulations that discriminated against women. The questionnaires primarily involved changes in language in statutes and regulations, such as the use of "chair" or "chairperson" instead of "chairman." My letter asked the governors to identify statutes, such as old-age benefit statutes that used "husband" instead of "spouse" when referring to those eligible.

I asked the governors to return their replies by May 1, 1984.

The New York Times, Sunday, June 3, 1984, reported that in a telegram sent to the Democratic governors' on May 24 by Lynn Cutler, then vice-chair of the Democratic National Committee, it said, "In this year of the gender gap, we don't want to assist the Republicans by allowing them to take credit for your work." She continued, "To enable us to prepare a Democratic response for the convention, I urge you to send the questionnaire to my office and inform the White House you are delaying your response."

Ms. Cutler said the Democratic response at the convention would "make clear that the work which has occurred in your state on behalf of women was done through your efforts and not those of the Reagan Administration."

Equality or Not?

The director of Governor Cuomo's Women's Division, Ronnie Eldridge, said that "true equality will not be achieved until the passage was won for an equal rights amendment to the [C]onstitution."

Governor O'Neill of Connecticut sent me a letter stating, "This office in no way wants the current Administration to receive credit for any progress our state has made in women's legal, economic or social status or anything we have accomplished despite Mr. Reagan."

I kept focused on my job. For me, just another day at the office.

I went to the Administration as a critic, recognizing that I would deal primarily with two groups that held President Reagan in less than high esteem.

Sometime later, Reagan signed the bill, making Dr. Martin Luther King's birthday a national holiday. Even though Reagan came from a poor background, he didn't support government intervention in the lives of its citizens.

Why Reagan? I disagreed with his predecessor, President Carter's action regarding the invasion by the Soviet Union into Afghanistan, and his answer to withdraw from the 1980 Olympics. There had to be a more effective way to handle Soviet communism. Nor did I support most of Reagan's policies, especially regarding voting rights. I viewed his opposition to the Civil Rights Act of 1964 and the Voting Rights Act of 1965 as an originalist interpretation of the Constitution's commitment to "secure the blessings of liberty to ourselves and our posterity" as long as that commitment did not include the enslaved black population that suffered the cruelty of chattel slavery.

But I strongly supported Reagan's approach to gender equity. After all, I was his approach. I had to believe in myself. Reagan believed in merit only, although he didn't spend time on what was meritorious or how it was achieved. This was the tide I was fighting against. If I went into a state where the Democratic governor would have been amenable to the 50 States Project, I would have political headwinds because it would benefit Reagan. If I went to a Republican governor, he (there was one female governor in 1982, Vesta Roy, R-New Hampshire) might have been reluctant to support gender equality.

Still, it was seen as something that would benefit the national party. However, there was no Federal money for the Project so states would have to bear its cost. This was a suicide mission. There were layers of opposition. I was a lightning rod. The mistake was that I was not a "window dressing" person. If given a task, I would make it work and make it palatable to be understood and supported by the most significant number of people. The Republicans chose the wrong person for the job they didn't want done.

I accepted the job, hoping to make a difference and prevent more bad policies toward women and blacks. At the beginning of the job, I didn't have a clear line of demarcation between my responsibilities and other staff. A Washington Post Style page headliner article on September 22, 1985, included the views of others. "According to some of [Trudi's] confidants, Morrison was constantly frustrated because 'she did not always have the complete green light' for her projects and had to battle intra-office jealousies and turf fights. Some of the jealousies directed at her, friends believed, were because she was an energetic doer who set a pace few could follow. Others, outside the staff, thought she was blind to a situation they saw as basically window dressing. 'Her exuberance is not always understood,' says one friend."

During a 50 States trip to Salt Lake City, Utah, in 1984, I was invited to a reception at the governor's house in my honor. Scott Matheson was the governor. I took a taxi rather than have a car pick me up. I was hoping for a mini-tour guide like cab drivers usually give. But this cab driver said nothing, even when I asked him questions. I sat back and enjoyed the sunset over one of the most beautiful cities I had ever seen.

We drove out of the city to an area where mansions thrived. These were not the mansions of the nouveau riche. They were

Equality or Not?

generational money. Even at night, the meticulously manicured lawns and specialty gardens competed with the mature trees lining the brick driveway pavers. The taxi driver stopped and pointed toward the mansion we stopped in front of.

I paid him, and he sped off. I looked at the estates on that block, but no lights were on. I was in high heels, walking up numerous stairs and around stately mansions, knocking on doors, and looking in windows. Finally, I noticed a foyer light in an estate three doors down from where the cab driver pointed. The gentleman of the mansion came to the door, and I quickly explained the situation.

He told me to come in and that he would make some calls. I asked if I could use the phone when he finished because I needed to call the White House. Even though it was after hours, I had a code to reach whomever I needed. I called Jim Baker, who advised me to stay where I was, and that he'd handle things from his end. Next, a man that I had never seen entered the mansion. He introduced himself as Orrin Hatch. Senator Hatch (R-UT) took me to a more excellent hotel than I was staying in.

The reception, in my honor, was canceled. I never met the governor. The governor's mansion wasn't on that block. They traced the cab and questioned the driver, who referred to me using the "N" word. The company fired the driver on the spot. Senator Hatch was so happy when I got my Senate appointment. He remained protective of me.

Jim Baker came to my aid a couple of times. For me, he was "Johnny on the Spot." I was taken aback when I heard he made inflammatory remarks about Jewish Americans. Was he a cobra ready to bite?

Allegedly, Baker was overheard saying, "F— the Jews, they vote 70%-90% for Democrats; they don't vote for us anyway."

Underneath my disappointment lay truisms that must be addressed. If a demographic group votes nearly 100% for one party, no matter what happens in the electorate or the real world, what's the incentive for the other side to court them?

WINNING THE BATTLE AGAINST MYSELF

Do most politicians think this? In my experience, people who think and speak of groups in monolithic terms about ethnicity, race, gender, and religion tend to objectify those same groups when they meet someone they like who is a member of one of those groups. We've all heard the "I have several black friends," "My childhood friends were black," or "When I look at you, I don't see color" comments.

Can you imagine in your wildest dreams that a president of our country, Donald Trump, would say "that Jews stick together" and are "only in it for themselves," the Washington Post reported, citing former and current senior officials? I read that quote in The Times of Israel on September 23, 2020. Reprehensible!

I flew into Orlando International Airport. Senator Paula Hawkins (R-FL) sent a car to pick me up. I was impressed.

Paula lived in the northeast section of Winter Park, Florida. The area had a suburban, urban feel. The city boasted bricked streets and elegant homes. The car that picked me up drove us to Paula's speech to the Log Cabin Republicans. She used the standard Republican talking points... building a strong economy, creating jobs, free enterprise, reducing oppressive tax rates, balancing the budget, and upholding international agreements. In the evening, Paula surprised me with Winter Park Bach Festival tickets. Music was informally combined with information about the composer. It was a delightful music experience.

On November 1, 1984, President Reagan wrote me the following:

> *Dear Trudi:*
> *The American people will judge our team's work in just a few days. I'm pleased to have this opportunity to render a judgment of my own and offer thanks for the invaluable assistance you've given me.*
> *[Discussion of achievements]*

Equality or Not?

I simply want you to know how much your fine performance has meant to me. For all you have accomplished—not only on my behalf but in the best interest of our nation—you have my lasting gratitude. From my heart, thank you, and God bless you.

Sincerely, Ronald Reagan

President Reagan was re-elected.

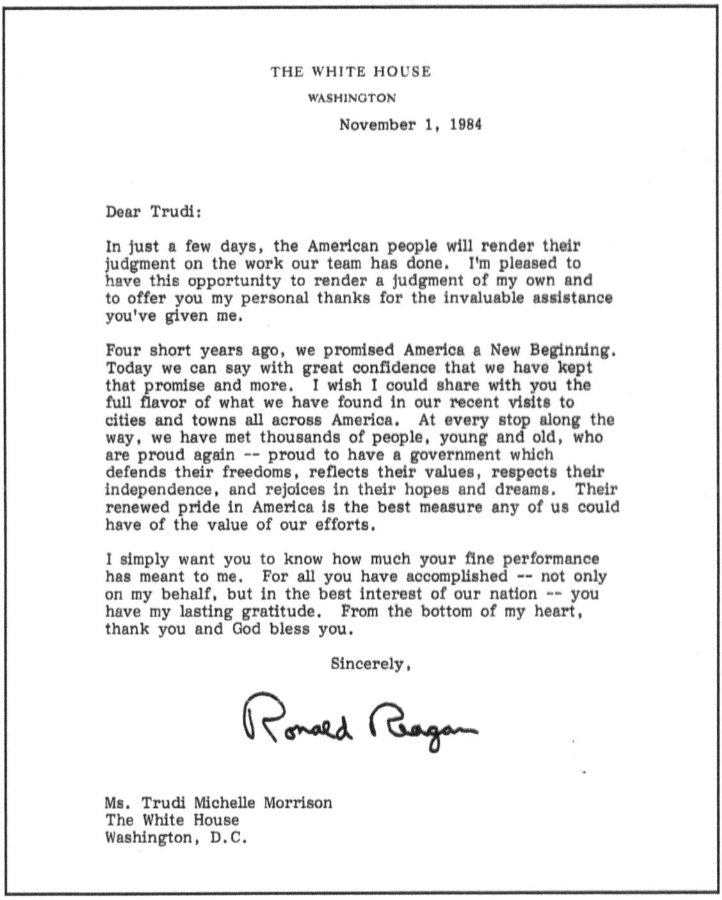

>
> THE WHITE HOUSE
> WASHINGTON
>
> November 1, 1984
>
> Dear Trudi:
>
> In just a few days, the American people will render their judgment on the work our team has done. I'm pleased to have this opportunity to render a judgment of my own and to offer you my personal thanks for the invaluable assistance you've given me.
>
> Four short years ago, we promised America a New Beginning. Today we can say with great confidence that we have kept that promise and more. I wish I could share with you the full flavor of what we have found in our recent visits to cities and towns all across America. At every stop along the way, we have met thousands of people, young and old, who are proud again -- proud to have a government which defends their freedoms, reflects their values, respects their independence, and rejoices in their hopes and dreams. Their renewed pride in America is the best measure any of us could have of the value of our efforts.
>
> I simply want you to know how much your fine performance has meant to me. For all you have accomplished -- not only on my behalf, but in the best interest of our nation -- you have my lasting gratitude. From the bottom of my heart, thank you and God bless you.
>
> Sincerely,
>
> Ronald Reagan
>
> Ms. Trudi Michelle Morrison
> The White House
> Washington, D.C.

Figure 22. -Letter from President Reagan.

WINNING THE BATTLE AGAINST MYSELF

Next came the Baker-Regan swap, and President Reagan appointed Pat Buchanan as the White House Communication Director and Linda Chavez as head of the Office of Public Liaison. Linda had staff conduct a phony exercise of writing papers explaining their jobs and justifying why they should be allowed to stay.

She pushed through an office reorganization, arguing that her White House door would remain open to hear the ideas and wishes of ethnic and racial groups.

Please... she was Mexican, and I was black. Tell that to someone else. She established three divisions: one for economic issues, a second for domestic matters, and a third for military problems. Ethnic, religious, and other interest groups were "clustered" in the three areas based on their interests. The new approach and placement of the liaison office under Buchanan raised suspicions that it was now more ideological. I didn't fit in this new configuration, so I was sure I would be let go. After chairing the first White House military briefing for minorities in May 1985, I returned to a 30-day firing notice.

Interestingly, a Washington Post story on page 3A, December 19, 1985, read:

"The conservative community is buzzing with questions about Linda Chavez, who not so long-ago switched parties and is now being pushed as a contender for the Republican Senate nomination in Maryland. The story is beginning to surface about the way Mrs. Chavez is swinging the personnel ax, chopping off the heads of loyal Reaganites in the White House office of public liaison, and packing the place with Democrats. Viewed from another perspective, observers find it strange that Mrs. Chavez is firing the women on her staff and replacing them with men. Senior White House officials are skirting a confrontation by urging her to run for the Senate."

Linda ran for the Senate and lost.

Chapter 16

The Palm

"I didn't get there by wishing for it or hoping for it, but by working for it."

- Estée Lauder

I hadn't met Senator Dole yet, but I met Elizabeth Dole as she was leaving the White House to become Secretary of Transportation, and I was coming in. Thelma introduced me to Mrs. Dole. I attended the National Prayer Breakfast in 1984 when Secretary Dole was selected to read from the New Testament. I received the same honor in 1986 when I got a call from Senator Lawton Chiles (R-Florida) asking me to read the New Testament at The 34th Annual National Prayer Breakfast on February 6, 1986, at the International Ballroom at the Washington Hilton Hotel. I was humbled.

The evening I left the White House, we ran into Senator Bob Dole and Secretary Elizabeth Dole at The Palm, a restaurant in Dupont Circle. I argued with my husband about spending money on an extravagant dinner when I had just been terminated with no job possibilities. He blew me off.

"You pay then," I said.

The Palm was where politicians, journalists, news anchors, civic leaders, movie stars, and writers frequented. The air buzzed

WINNING THE BATTLE AGAINST MYSELF

with the clinking of glasses and the low hum of important conversations. The aroma of sizzling steaks and fresh seafood wafted through the air, making my mouth water despite my earlier protests about the cost. The walls were crammed with cartoons and caricatures of its famous guests. The food was spectacular, especially the lobster tails and steaks.

"Please join us," Secretary Dole said.

"Thank you so much. Are you sure it wouldn't be an imposition?"

"Of course not."

"Don't order drinks," I whispered to my husband. He gave me a strange look.

A waiter approached, "Still or sparkling?"

"Still," Senator Dole said.

I always ordered the 1/2 Broiled 3 lb. Nova Scotia Lobster and a side of leaf spinach. New York Cheesecake was my dessert.

Vernon Jordan came over to the table to pay respects to the Doles. Mr. Jordan headed the National Urban League and the United Negro College Fund and became an influential counselor in political and business circles. Vernon Jordan and Senator Dole were affiliated with Akin Gump, the Washington law and lobbying firm.

"Hi, I'm Vernon," he said, extending his hand.

"Nice meeting you, Mr. Jordan. I'm Trudi Morrison."

He pulled up a chair and turned to me. "May I get you a drink?"

"No, thank you, but thanks for asking."

Mr. Jordan leaned over and said something to Senator Dole.

"Take care, Trudi," he said, walking away from the table.

The following day, my friend Cathi Villalpando called to tell me she and the Sergeant at Arms of the Senate, Ernie Garcia, had discussed the deputy position. Ernie was recently named Sergeant at Arms, becoming the first Hispanic to hold the post. Ernie was from Kansas, Senator Dole's home state. I heard that Thelma Duggin, my friend who worked with Elizabeth Dole at

The Palm

the White House and the Department of Transportation, was the leading contender for the deputy position. Thelma was the person who introduced me to Elizabeth Dole and the person who called me from the Republican National Committee when I had the incident with Senator Thad Cochran while I was in the White House. Cathi was my ardent supporter and urged Ernie to stand by me with Senator Dole.

Chapter 17

What Happened?

> *"The woman who can create her own job is the woman who will win fame and fortune."*
>
> **-Amelia Earhart**

Jobless in June 1985, I sat at home contemplating my next steps and eating bonbons while watching my butt and stomach expand as the days dragged on. I had offers from five Federal departments; they could not have been less appealing. Unemployed and no attractive job offers?—I had some audacity.

The phone rang, and the woman at the other end said, "Senator Dole wants to see you."

Shocked, I asked, "When?"

"As soon as possible."

It was raining cats and dogs. My husband had the car.

I put the bonbons down and rushed to the bedroom. Most of my clothes were still in cleaning bags since I had nowhere to wear them. I called a taxi and started to get dressed.

Why does Senator Dole want to see me? Should I wear a dark suit or a colorful light-weight suit? Do I have any money? I heard the cab driver honk. I zipped the side of my gray suit skirt, grabbed my jacket and purse, and set the alarm.

What Happened?

The traffic was abysmal. The cab waited impatiently for three minutes to merge from I-395 South onto the 14th Street Bridge. We were only 1.25 miles from the entrance to the 14th Street Bridge from I-395 South to the U.S. Capitol, but traffic was stagnant. We finally crept to Independence Avenue, S.W. Independence, and 14th Street, which was 1.4 miles from the Capitol and usually took 6 minutes. It took us 25 minutes.

I felt panic rising in me. I sat on the edge of the backseat, willing the traffic to move and the driver to go faster. I felt a bit of sweat under my arms. Did I put on deodorant? I asked the driver to turn left and go up Constitution Avenue instead.

Constitution Avenue was bumper-to-bumper traffic. I hopped out of the taxi into the drenching rain and started running toward the Constitution Avenue and Delaware entrance to the Capitol.

The hill was steep and slippery. I stumbled and broke the heel of my left shoe. I took both shoes off and continued running in my stocking feet, using my briefcase as an umbrella.

After clearances, I got to Senator Dole's office, and his secretaries looked at me with astonishment. Mascara ran down my cheeks, and makeup melted off my face. One of the secretaries asked what size shoe I wore; the other secretary told me that Senator Dole was still on the floor for an unexpected vote. She handed me a box of tissues and walked me to the nearest restroom.

I took off my shredded pantyhose and reapplied makeup as best I could. My hair was a loss; nothing would help it. It was bushing out by the millisecond.

The first secretary met me in the hallway and handed me a pair of kitten heels. I forced myself not to ask who the shoes belonged to, whether I could use footies, or if the owner had athlete's feet. Just put the shoes on, Trudi, I said to myself; athlete's foot won't kill you. Desperation can make you shut up.

They put me in Senator Dole's private office. Senator Dole finally came and sat next to me. We exchanged views on various subjects in a surprisingly laid-back way.

WINNING THE BATTLE AGAINST MYSELF

"Have you and Mrs. Dole been to Sardi's in New York City? It has Broadway celebrities on its walls as caricatures, similar to The Palm in Washington, which has a cartoon of you and Mrs. Dole on the wall," I asked.

"We've been there, but don't have a chance to get out of Washington very often. Do you want to work in the Senate in a law enforcement role?"

Jobless and approaching financial ruin, I said yes.

As I sat there, acutely aware of my disheveled appearance and borrowed shoes, I marveled at the strange twists of fate that had brought me to this moment. From unemployment to potentially making history—all in the span of a rainy afternoon.

"When can you start?"

"Tomorrow."

"Since tomorrow is Saturday, why don't we wait until Monday?"

That evening at dinner at The Palm, Senator Dole excitedly said to his wife, Elizabeth, "I've just made history today."

And yes, it was a history-making moment for a person of color and a woman, shattering the status quo for people of color and women. Previously, only white men had received the honor. As Dr. Martin Luther King, Jr. stated, "The arc of the moral universe is long, but it bends toward justice."

In July 1985, I became Deputy Sergeant at Arms of the United States Senate, the first female and the first person of color.

The Sergeant and Deputy Sergeant at Arms worked as a team. The Senate elected the Sergeant at Arms and was the Senate's Chief law enforcement officer. In this role, we had ceremonial functions that developed through custom and precedent, such as escorting the president and other heads of state or official guests of the Senate who are attending official functions in the Capitol, making arrangements for funerals of senators who die in office, assisting in plans for the inauguration of the president, organizing the swearing-in and orientation programs for newly elected senators, escorting the senators as they

What Happened?

proceed from the Senate to the House Chamber for the State of the Union Address or joint sessions or meetings of Congress, and other times when the Senate moves as a body. By custom, the Sergeant at Arms was the custodian of the Senate gavel.

As Deputy Sergeant at Arms and Chief Operating Officer of the Senate, I was appointed by the Senate Majority Leader, Bob Dole. I commanded 2,200 employees from Capitol Hill buildings to senatorial offices in the 50 states. It wasn't long before my appointment that blacks were finally allowed to wait tables in the private dining room (if waiting tables in an August body is considered an achievement).

Now, here I was, eating in the dining room and bringing guests to the dining room. When I was at the White House, I took as many people of color as I could to the Mess for lunch; here, at the Senate, I hosted as many minority friends as possible in the Senate Dining Room.

I was also responsible for providing computer and technology support services, video and audio recording services, photographic services, printing and graphic services, and telecommunications services to the Senate, assisting Senate offices with the management of their staffing, mailing, purchasing, leasing, and financial accounting needs, providing continuity of operations and emergency preparedness training and assistance to the Senate community, issuing staff I.D.s, arranging for parking and issuing parking permits, arranging cleaning and furnishing Senate offices in the Capitol, greeting and directing visitors with official business in the Capitol, credentialing and assisting members of news media who cover the Senate, and administering the Senate Page Program.

My starting salary was $75,000, a salary reported in Jet magazine on August 19, 1985, equal to Secretary Samuel Pierce's (the only black cabinet member's) salary. The job also came with a telephone-equipped car and two drivers, Willie and Eugene. Although it was public information, my mother wasn't pleased with an article mentioning my salary. She told me to have Jet

WINNING THE BATTLE AGAINST MYSELF

Magazine retract the money part of the article. She said she didn't want people to think I had money.

Mommy was always one who abhorred elitism. She despised braggadocious people. She tried to hold onto fundamental values and not have us appear to have more than anyone else. She was frugal and raised on a farm, although she married into a reasonably well-off family. When church members commented to her about my salary, she played it off, saying, "You can't believe everything you read in magazines." One article claimed I owned a villa in Montego Bay, Jamaica. Mommy called the magazine directly and told them off. They didn't retract the article.

Figure 23. -Ernie Garcia-Sergeant at Arms, Trudi, Senator Bill Armstrong (R-CO), Senator Bob Dole. June 12, 1985. Credit: U.S. Senate Historical Office

Chapter 18

Hold The Line

"Standing in the middle of the road is very dangerous; you get knocked down by the traffic from both sides."
-Margaret Thatcher

Senator Dole invited senators to meet me. All Republican senators came; a few Democrat senators showed up. The senators were given name tags with names, party affiliations, and states on them. One man kept going to the back of the line whenever another senator appeared. I kept wondering who that man was and why he was doing that. The line finally ended, so the mystery man was the last man standing and wasn't wearing a name tag. The mysterious one shook my hand and walked away.

I turned to Senator Dole and asked who that man was. He said, "Thad Cochran from Mississippi."

Say what?! Cochran had carried the White House incident and me in his head for years! It was too silly for me even to be flattered or insulted.

This moment encapsulated the complex dynamics I would navigate in my new role - a world where old prejudices lingered beneath the surface of polite political interactions.

There were good times at the Senate. I had a grand welcoming reception hosted by former Senator Ed Brooke

WINNING THE BATTLE AGAINST MYSELF

(R-Massachusetts), the only black senator who has held his seat since Reconstruction, and HUD Cabinet Secretary Samuel Pierce. Food was prepared by the celebrated chef, Mr. K, for upward of 400 leaders and supporters.

The Congressional Record on February 24, 1986, recorded Senator Dole saying, "Mr. President, in 1926, Dr. Carter Woodson, founder of the Association for the Study of Afro-American Life and History, initiated the first formal tribute to black Americans by establishing Negro History Week. This event has since become an annual tradition, and this year, we have designated the month of February as Black History Month. In celebrating Black history, I feel it is especially important to draw attention to the contributions made by Blacks in the Senate. I take great pride in the fact that the three Black Members of the Senate [Hiram Revels in 1870, Blanche Kelso Bruce in 1874, and Edward William Brooke in 1967] have been Republicans. I am also honored to have had the opportunity to appoint the first Black, Trudi Michelle Morrison, as the Senate's deputy sergeant at arms."

It was 16 years later, in 2001, before another black became an Officer, Alfonso Lenhardt, as Sergeant at Arms. In 2003, Dr. Barry Black was the first black Senate Chaplain. Eighteen years passed before another black was elected the first Secretary of the Senate, Sonceria Ann Berry, making her only the second black woman since my appointment 36 years earlier.

Bob Dole was committed to the conscientious enforcement of laws enacted to remedy past discrimination. Senator Dole supported the 1964 Civil Rights Act, the 1965 Voting Rights Act, and the extension of the Voting Rights Act in 1982. He voted for the 1967 Age Discrimination in Employment Act and fought for the passage of the Americans with Disabilities Act.

In World War II, he suffered life-threatening wounds, leaving him with limited mobility in his right arm and a numb left arm. Senator Dole's grievous battle wounds in Italy and others led him to almost single-handedly raise hundreds of millions of dollars in private donations for the World War II Memorial in Washington, DC.

Like Daddy, Senator Dole was among the greatest of the Greatest Generation. Senator Dole enjoyed sports, so I brought Marvin Hagler, Sugar Ray Leonard, Tommy Hearns, David Robinson, and his father, Ambrose to meet him. He quipped he had never seen so many senators show up, even when a vote was on the floor.

Senator Dole's humor was legendary. We also shared a love of vanilla ice cream. When the Senate Dining Room staff brought us ice cream, I watched Senator Dole drain off the melted portions; he only liked the frozen part. I wanted all of it. Our birthdays were three days apart; he was on July 22, and mine was on July 25. Ice cream was colder and sweeter on those days with him.

Unbeknownst to most, Senator Dole was a kind, compassionate man. He believed in giving second chances. The man I knew was selfless and thought that people were innately good.

Not only did Senator Dole empower women, but he also married one of the most accomplished women I know.

Elizabeth Dole graduated with distinction as a Phi Beta Kappa from Duke University. She received a Master of Arts in Teaching and a law degree from Harvard. When I met Mrs. Dole, she left her White House post as Assistant to President Reagan for Public Liaison, and I was starting my White House tenure. Elizabeth was the first woman appointed U.S. Secretary of Transportation and later as U.S. Secretary of Labor. She was the second woman to head the American Red Cross since 1881, when Clara Barton founded the organization. Mrs. Dole ran for President and became the first female U.S. Senator from North Carolina.

Senator Bob Dole loved the U.S. Capitol. Most of all, he loved our country. Senator Dole viewed public service as one of the most honorable professions.

Chapter 19

Cruelty

*"If They Come For Me In The Morning,
They Will Come For You In The Night."*
-Angela Davis (1971)
(Voices of the Resistance)

In a cruel twist of fate, one of my first official duties as Deputy Sergeant at Arms was to escort Members to the funeral of former Mississippi Senator James Eastland, an avowed racist who staunchly opposed civil rights legislation. As chair of the judiciary committee for 22 years, Eastland prevented civil rights bills from being considered before the full Senate.

In June 1964, three civil rights workers — James Chaney, 21, Andrew Goodman, 24, and Michael Schwerner, 20 — went missing in Mississippi. They had been pulled over for alleged speeding, arrested, and released earlier that night. Then they were gone. President Lyndon B. Johnson called Eastland for counsel. The call from the Oval Office was recorded, and the audio is available at the University of Virginia's Miller Center.

"Jim, we got three kids missing down there. What can I do about it?"

"Well, I don't know. I don't believe there are three missing. I believe it's a publicity stunt." Eastland told Johnson it was fake news.

Cruelty

The three were found six weeks later buried in a mud dam. All three had been shot; Chaney had been tortured before being killed. Mississippi authorities did as little as possible to bring those responsible to justice. They charged 18 men with depriving the three of their civil rights. Seven were convicted.

One of the acquitted, Edgar Ray Killen, was a KKK leader who killed the three men. Killen was found guilty of manslaughter on June 21, 2005, 41 years after the men were killed.

Eastland was called the "Voice of the White South" and the "Godfather of Mississippi Politics." He often said black people were "an inferior race." He served in the Senate for 35 years and died on February 19, 1986. And here I was, the first black and first woman Officer of the United States Senate, two groups Eastland despised, escorting his casket.

If Frederick Douglass had been alive, he would have responded to Eastland's claim that black people were "an inferior race" to most of us. Douglass would have said to Eastland, "I am a man!"

Douglass used himself as an example, arguing for his humanity to argue for the humanity of blacks and, therefore, our right to be treated equally under the Constitution. It was a sad commentary on America that a man with Douglass's intellect must repeatedly proclaim himself a human being. But he did so for the sake of many others who faced the same prejudice but could not argue for themselves.

As I navigated my role in the Senate, I encountered several other senators with histories of supporting segregation. Strom Thurmond, Jesse Helms, Robert Byrd, and John Stennis each had their own record of opposing civil rights. Their reactions to my presence ranged from curt nods to outright ignorance. Helms and Byrd never spoke to me, even when I offered morning greetings. Stennis once rushed past me, knocking me off balance without an apology. These interactions served as stark reminders of the progress we had made—and the long road still ahead.

WINNING THE BATTLE AGAINST MYSELF

In October 1986, I learned the best political lesson not taught in books.

Senator Dole asked me to determine what the civil rights leaders thought about South Africa's Apartheid and their opinions on how he should vote. I don't recall if Senator Dole had black staff, but it was a trial balloon, and he thought I was the person to float it. Perhaps he asked me to carry out this task because he and I had discussed how apartheid affected every facet of life in a country locked in centuries-old patterns of discrimination and racism.

Senator Dole told me he staunchly opposed apartheid by the South African government. He implied that President Reagan would put aside his reservations and sign a bill penalizing South Africa for its racial policies if congressional negotiators limited economic sanctions to those approved by the Senate.

I called the Southern Christian Leadership Conference leaders I knew: Coretta Scott King, Rev. Joseph Lowery, Ben Hooks, Randall Robinson, Ralph Abernathy, and Julian Bond. My friend, Julian, called Bayard Rustin and Fred Shuttlesworth.

President Reagan vetoed a measure that would impose economic sanctions against South Africa's racist system of apartheid. The Reagan Administration had sought to impose economic restrictions under a presidential executive order. However, opponents, including 81 House Republicans, insisted that the approach failed to go far enough.

In responding to the congressional action, Reagan said:

"[The] ... vote should not be viewed as the final chapter in America's efforts, along with our allies, to address the plight of the people of South Africa. Instead, it underscores that America—and that means all of us—opposes apartheid, a malevolent and archaic system alien to our ideals. The debate was not about whether or not to oppose apartheid but, instead, how best to fight it and bring freedom to that troubled country.

Punitive sanctions are not the best course of action; they hurt the people they are intended to help. I hope these disciplinary

Cruelty

sanctions do not lead to more violence and repression. Our administration will, nevertheless, implement the law. However, it must be recognized that this will not solve the serious problems plaguing that country. The United States must also move forward with positive measures to encourage peaceful change and advance the cause of democracy in South Africa..."

Senator Dole first supported sanctions in August 1986. But Senator Dole was a loyalist, a conforming trait. Congress overrode Reagan's veto, putting the sanctions into place, but not before Reagan convinced several senators of his point of view.

The Philadelphia Inquirer listed them: "Thad Cochran of Mississippi, Robert Dole of Kansas, Orrin G. Hatch of Utah, Don Nickles of Oklahoma, Alan K. Simpson of Wyoming, Ted Stevens of Alaska, and Barry Goldwater of Arizona."

Two years after that vote in the Senate—Reagan demanded that Mandela be released from prison.

We should never be surprised by what politicians do; we should never make it so they disappoint us; politicians will do and say anything to stay in power. By asking me to make these calls, Senator Dole was either indecisive or decisive since he planned to run for President in 1988, a fact I didn't know then. He could have put me in a bad situation by taking a risk for which the civil rights leaders and the senators held me responsible. It was a considerable risk; I could have ended up in the middle. The Comprehensive Anti-Apartheid Act was passed on October 2, 1986.

Chapter 20

Let's Build Something

"The facts of life are that a child who has seen war cannot be compared with a child who doesn't know what war is except from television."
-Sophia Loren

The Mike Mansfield (D-Montana) room was bombed in November 1983. Mansfield was the longest-serving Senate Majority Leader and served from 1961 to 1977. A group calling itself the Armed Resistance Unit claimed credit for the bombing, which caused an estimated $300,000 in damage. Thankfully, no one was injured.

The group was organized and led by women. Women picked the targets, made the bombs, and implanted the devices. The United States military involvement in Lebanon and Grenada motivated the group.

In October 1983, the United States invaded the island nation of Grenada and replaced the ruling New Jewel Movement with the previous parliamentary government. Following a five-year investigation of the bombing, Federal agents arrested six group members in May 1988 and charged them with bombing the Capitol.

Let's Build Something

The 1983 bombing catalyzed stringent security measures in and outside the Capitol. As a result of the attack, areas previously open to the public at the Capitol were closed, and staff identification cards were instituted.

I came to the Senate two years after the bombing. The aftermath of the bombing marked a significant shift in my responsibilities. Suddenly, the abstract concept of security became a tangible, urgent priority. Each day brought new challenges as we balanced the need for openness in a democratic institution with the imperative of protecting the people within its walls.

I worked closely with the Committee on Senate Rules and Administration and the Architect of the Capitol, George White, a Federal employee, toward active and consistent engagement in new security measures and the approval of the security-related devices installed in the Capitol buildings and the surrounding Senate office buildings. We installed additional metal detectors.

I remember the day we activated the new metal detectors. As I watched senators and staffers file through, some grumbling about the inconvenience, I felt a mix of pride and unease. We were making the Capitol safer.

Can you imagine my sadness viewing President Trump's Capitol insurrection on January 6, 2021?

Our efforts focused on life safety, emergency preparedness, and Capitol security. As part of these efforts, we developed and explored new technologies and accelerated efforts to ensure the continuity of legislative and constituent service operations. For example, we created automatic fail-over capabilities to ensure that critical systems and current data were available anytime there was a failure at the Senate campus. We also provided that off-site capabilities were available to Member offices to afford them protection when their systems failed or when they failed or when they could not access the system while they were dislocated from their current offices.

WINNING THE BATTLE AGAINST MYSELF

When I started at the Senate, I didn't know where the bathroom was when I was on the floor. I found Senator Paula Hawkins (R-Florida), one of two female Senators, and asked her where the bathroom was. She said there was no restroom close to the Senate chambers. I couldn't believe it. Senators Hawkins, Senator Nancy Kassabaum (R-Kansas), and I had to go upstairs to use the facilities. I later had a bathroom constructed for women near chambers. As of this writing, the Senate has twenty-five female senators, none of whom are black. The simple act of adding a women's restroom near the chambers symbolized the gradual, often overlooked ways in which the institution was slowly changing. Each small step forward carried the weight of decades of exclusion and the promise of a more inclusive future.

On January 28, 1986, seventy-three minutes into the flight, the space shuttle Challenger blew up. All the astronauts were killed. I later read that the investigation determined that the disaster was caused by the failure of an "O-ring" seal in one of the two solid-fuel rockets.

I didn't know what that meant, but I remember that day vividly. I was sitting in my Senate office with the television broadcasting the lift-off. The explosion was shocking.

I went to Senator Dole's office to see if he needed me to do anything. He had just placed a call to President Reagan. Senator Dole seemed stunned. Most people never saw the compassionate side of Senator Dole. He was a man who felt things deeply. His feelings were not demonstrative, leaving many to misinterpret his need to suffer and grieve privately.

I was there when they spoke and agreed that the President would delay the State of the Union speech scheduled for that evening out of respect. It was the first time a president had delayed the yearly address.

By early 1986, Majority Leader Bob Dole and Democratic Leader Robert C. Byrd worried that the lack of television coverage transformed the Senate into the nation's forgotten legislative body. House members were becoming far more visible

Let's Build Something

than senators to their constituents. The two leaders eventually engineered a vote in which the Senate agreed to a three-month trial period, with live national coverage to begin on June 2, 1986. The Senate voted to make this coverage permanent. It fell to our office and the Architect of the Capitol to usher in televised Senate proceedings on C-SPAN 2.

I was actively involved in ushering in televised Senate proceedings. Work began on strengthening, renovating, and preserving the West Front of the U.S. Capitol in 1983. Structural problems developed over the years because of defects in the original foundations, deterioration of the sandstone-facing material, and alterations to the basic building fabric because of fire.

During my tenure from 1985 to 1987, over 1,000 stainless steel tie rods were set into the building's masonry to strengthen the structure. Over 30 layers of paint were removed, and damaged stonework was repaired or replicated. Ultimately, 40 percent of the sandstone blocks were replaced with limestone. The walls were treated with a special consolidant and then painted to match the marble wings. The project was completed in 1987, well ahead of schedule and under budget.

Meanwhile, my non-technical responsibilities included deciding on the color of draperies, setting soft gradations so the senators wouldn't notice how bright the light was getting, hiring make-up artists to powder bald heads to lessen glare off their heads and carpet color.

By 1986, Senator William L. Armstrong (R-CO) convinced his colleagues to allow cameras onto the Senate floor. C-SPAN2 followed C-SPAN on June 2, 1986, when the U.S. Senate permitted itself to be televised. As the cameras rolled for the first time, I felt a mix of excitement and apprehension. We were opening the Senate to unprecedented public scrutiny. I couldn't help but wonder how this newfound transparency would shape the future of our democracy. C-SPAN2 began full-time operations on January 5, 1987.

Chapter 21

Unfair

"I think that racism is ugly and so unfair, and I believe that we all need one another."

-Ruby Bridges

(In the 1960s, by the age of six years; Ruby became the first black child to desegregate the all-white William Frantz Elementary School in New Orleans).

In February 1986, every member of Congress was considered an at-will employee, meaning they had no contractual or statutory grant of tenure. They were virtually terminable at will, and as a general rule, were not legally entitled to any due process procedures concerning the removal and/or other disciplinary actions. At that time, an originalist interpretation of the Constitution prevailed for firing employees.

Explanation: The originalist interpretation of the constitutional text viewed it through the lens of historical context, rather than considering a more modern understanding of the society. According to this interpretation, Article II of the Constitution granted the president inherent authority to fire Federal employees. As a result, any legislation establishing employee rights, such as civil service laws, was deemed unconstitutional. Consequently, employees were left without a proper mechanism to address their concerns and Congress granted itself exemptions from various civil rights, labor, as well as workplace safety and health laws that protected employees in the private sector and the executive branch.

I was informed that the Senate Service Department had ethical and performance issues.

The responsibility of firing the employees fell on me, which became the most challenging task of my career.

I obtained approval from Senator Dole for every aspect of the task, sending him notes with a "Yes" or "No" box to check. I also sought the opinion of the esteemed Senate Deputy General Counsel, Ken Benjamin.

Six of the twenty-one terminated staffers sued me for $25 million in the U.S. Federal court. The staffers contended that their dismissals were due to sex and age discrimination. I asked Senator Dole to hold hearings, which were held on Capitol Hill in July, regarding the allegations of brutal findings and false charges about character and job performance.

The case was dismissed and the suit was deemed frivolous. Senator Dole, Deputy General Counsel Benjamin, and I collaborated on a draft of protective Federal employment laws similar to those provided to executive branch employees. It took ten more years before that revised draft turned into Congress's Congressional Accountability Act of 1995. During my tenure at the Administrative Office of the United States Courts, I discussed this legislation in this book.

In 2020, there was a presidential election, which resulted in the removal of incumbent President Donald Trump. After a presidential election, it is necessary to certify the results as per the Constitution. A peaceful transition of power is the bedrock of our society.

Instead, President Trump incited an armed insurrection in the U.S. Capitol on January 6, 2021. Despite previously stating that he would join the terrorists, he fled the scene. This disturbing event displayed a dangerous expression of anger.

WINNING THE BATTLE AGAINST MYSELF

Subsequently, Trump secluded himself in the White House for six days as he descended into another level of madness.

People who stormed the Capitol carried Trump flags and chanted "Hang Mike Pence," the vice president in the Capitol, certifying the presidential election. Destruction, sedition, treason, theft, assault, and an attempted coup. Rioters infiltrated the Capitol's basement tunnels, overtook the Rotunda, and breached the double doors. There was pure chaos. If I were still Deputy Sergeant at Arms, I fear that my race and gender would have put an even bigger target on my back.

Democracy progressed as President Trump was impeached by the House of Representatives for the second time during his final days in office. The charge against him was "incitement of insurrection" relating to the attack on the U.S. Capitol.

This unfortunate event resulted in over 140 police officers being injured, one woman losing her life, and four officers tragically taking their own lives. Personally, I felt a sense of relief that I was not fulfilling my Senate duties on January 6, 2021. In the insurrection's aftermath, I reached out to Senator Dole to express my relief about our absence and to discuss our hypothetical actions had we been present.

He was disheartened, to put it mildly.

"This is awful. It's unimaginable. I had trouble watching it. Are you alright?"

"I'm pretty shaken. The United States Capitol was occupied by rioters and looters!"

"It is our symbol of democracy. It's also the place we go to work every day."

"Exactly. Senator, did you know slaves were told that they could earn their freedom by earning wages while working on the Capitol project for six years? I have never heard or read that any enslaved African earned freedom for their work on the Capitol."

"I don't remember specific details, but Maryland had a sizable free black population. Baltimore had the largest free black

Unfair

population in the country, so both enslaved and free men of color provided much of the labor used to build the Capitol."

"And now, those who call themselves patriots and profess to love America are destroying the Capitol and hurting people. What do you think we would have done, Senator Dole?"

"I'm not sure." He paused, breathing deeply. "I hope we would have acted upon the prior intelligence, adequately prepared, and declared a state of emergency to get outside law enforcement help."

"Well, I kinda missed the good ole' days when I was one of two people with the authority to arrest the President of the United States."

Senator Dole died on December 5, 2021.

Chapter 22

Crimson Leaves

"And all the lives we ever lived and all the lives to be are full of trees and changing leaves."

-Virginia Woolf

My husband secured a position as Deputy Mayor to Mayor Coleman Young in Detroit, Michigan in 1989. Despite being away from Washington, President Reagan appointed me to the Council of the Administrative Conference of the United States. Chief Justice Warren Burger swore me in. The Conference was an independent Federal agency charged with convening expert representatives from the public and private sectors to recommend administrative processes and procedures. The Council was responsible for calling plenary sessions, proposing bylaws, and regulations for the adoption made by the Assembly, reviewing budgetary proposals and approving the appointment of public members, and conducting research studies. There was no salary, but I had to fly back to Washington for meetings.

Living in Detroit was a different experience. Our apartment in Riverfront combined two apartments and had a stunning view of the Detroit River overlooking Toronto. We'd drive over the bridge and through customs to frequent the city's outstanding restaurants; some of the best food I ever had was in Toronto, Canada.

Figure 24. -Warren Earl Burger, Chief Justice of the United States Swearing In (June 6, 1988) Trudi Michelle Morrison to the Administrative Conference of the U.S..

However, I needed something to do other than going to the beauty shop in Riverfront every other day and eating like a horse. After all, how many times a week did I need a manicure or pedicure? And how many pants with elastic waists did I need? Time would pass anyway, so why not do something productive with it? I decided to go back to school for a terminal degree, a PhD.

We drove up to Ann Arbor to look around the University of Michigan. The Fall wind gusts gathered the red, yellow, purple, brown, crimson, and gold leaves and spread them unevenly across the ground in thousands of shapes. I found the rustling leaves warm and comfortable. The colors made me feel excited, like a child. I'd entered a cycle of growth and harvest.

Graduate schools require the Graduate Record Examination, an achievement test that measures your knowledge and skill level in a particular field of study. Mathematics was one of the fields tested. Not many forty-year-olds remember anything about math, except that they hated it. To make it a further unattainable dream, my husband purchased a Peugeot with a manual transmission that required the clutch to be pressed for each shift throughout the drive. My lessons in college with Rich Witkin's Camaro faded like a bad trip. This was the time of VHS (Video Home Systems) that played videos rented out from video stores. Long before Blockbuster Video, there was Erol's Video Club. Every day I ventured out in the Peugeot, jerking, stopping, running red lights so I didn't have to stop heading to Erol's to rent a tape on mathematics.

Day One I jerked to Erol's to rent a tape on Calculus; Day Two I started and stopped on a major thoroughfare to return Calculus and rent Trigonometry; Day Three, in the slowest traffic lane jerking and stalling—Statistics and Probability; Day Four grinding the gears, Geometry, which found the Erol's manager waiting for me with Basic Geometry and Algebra videos so I didn't have to stop; Day Five the manager ran alongside the car greeting me with a GED (General Educational Development) video.

Shockingly, I was one of three people who took admission that season.

The Michigan campus thrived with ivy-laden stone buildings. At age 40, I decided to apply to the Rackham Graduate School of Political Science at the University of Michigan, known for having the best political science program in the country. The winters in Ann Arbor were harsh on my 40-year-old body, as were the un-ending, heavily worn marble staircases.

After my dissertation defense, my committee chair wrote, "She was able to use her legal training to analyze materials that were crucial for understanding questions in political theory, and in doing so, she was able to bridge between law and theory fields in the discipline. I wanted to nominate the dissertation for the Corwin Prize from the American Political Science Association, but she thought that she was not heading into an academic career."

Crimson Leaves

I questioned one overarching truth in earning my PhD. What was philosophy? Did it ask what exists? How did I know what exists? What did I do about what exists? Regardless of what philosophy was; I absorbed the thoughts of the best thinkers in the philosophical neighborhood. And I discovered, with the help of my brilliant professor, Daniela Gobetti, that law and philosophy are deeply intertwined and inherently related.

Although I attended Michigan after my Senate tenure, I recognized that morality and belief need to be clarified about what should be considered the law in our world. Watching and listening to the Senate Majority Leader, Bob Dole, I understood that there were many arguments and debates about some of the most personal bills like abortion, gay rights, etc. While the law is the law, it is the process of becoming a law where philosophy must come into play rather than morality and belief. (Van Norman Law, Scottsdale, Arizona).

My husband's tenure in Detroit was unexpectedly cut short, so we made the decision to return to Washington. Despite the significant accomplishments I had achieved in my previous jobs, I found myself unemployed again, with no prospective employers showing interest.

In the meantime, my husband managed to secure a few consulting opportunities here and there.

Christmas was a week away, and we were short on food, including milk, for our six-month-old son, Logan. Fortunately, we had a kind neighbor who owned a real estate company, and he and his wife often invited us to their home. On Christmas week, I walked across the street and rang their doorbell. They gave me a warm welcome and I humbly asked our neighbor if there was any way I could help him at his company during the holidays. They allowed me to work as a receptionist at their real estate company and paid me thirty-five dollars. Fortunately, Logan had food, clothes, and toys for Christmas.

Chapter 23
Irony

"I have survivor skills. Some of that is superficial - what I present to people outwardly - but what makes people resilient is the ability to find humor and irony in situations that would otherwise overpower you."

-Amy Tan

In 1997, an irony occurred: I was tasked with implementing the Congressional Accountability Act of 1995 (CAA), which Senator Dole and I had paved the way for in the Senate in 1985, and it was now my full-time job in the third branch of government.

The judiciary, like Congress, had exempted itself from most Federal workplace protections and employee rights and prevented judges and other high-level judicial branch officials, including the Supreme Court justices and their law clerks, from being investigated and penalized for acts of sexual harassment and discrimination. The courts didn't have to play by the rules, they were adjudicating for others.

The CAA required legislative and judicial branch entities to follow many of the same employment and workplace safety laws applied to businesses. Little did the Administrative Office of the United States Courts (AO) or the judges know who the

Irony

person was that would be responsible for implementing the Congressional Plan. Those same laws came with me from the legislative branch. Once again, they hired the wrong person for the job they didn't want done.

It wasn't until 2001 when Senators Mazie Hirono (HI), Sheldon Whitehouse (RI), Patty Murray (WA), and Richard J. Durbin (IL), co-sponsored the Judiciary Accountability Act. This act applied to judicial branch employee laws that prohibit discrimination based on race, color, religion, sex (including sexual orientation or gender identity), national origin, age, or disability. Further, the bill prohibited retaliation against whistleblowers within the judicial branch. Their legislation did not apply to the Supreme Court justices or its law clerks.

I started teaching American Government and Politics at American University in 1995. I began my tenure at the AO in June 1997 while also continuing as an Associate Professor at American University.

On October 8, 1997, the AO Director established a Fair Employment Practices Office for me through his memorandum. This office was responsible for ensuring equal employment opportunity and resolving employment dispute resolution functions as its own office. Producing an annual statistical report for the judiciary required expertise to frame hypotheses, gather data, analyze, and put problems in manageable statistical and verbal form. Philosophical thinking and legal training strongly emphasized the precise formulation of ideas and issues. I was also able to formulate and solve problems, generate ideas for various issues, uncover hidden assumptions, and articulate alternative perspectives that had been overlooked. Although I did not have the authority to enforce Federal laws, I would have taught judges and court executives to take unfamiliar views or novel options seriously.

I could summarize complicated materials without undue simplification. I could integrate diverse data and construct helpful analogies. I could distinguish subtle differences without overlooking similarities. I could teach employment dispute resolution to the brightest legal minds in the country.

But I needed all my education, political acumen, and "gifts" to survive the treachery of the AO, an agency within the Federal government's judicial branch, and the arrogance of some Federal judges. Not a single day passed without a reminder of my race and gender as a black woman.

Throughout my career, I faced various comments that belittled and undermined me. I was told that my hair looked better when straightened rather than embracing its natural texture. People mistook me for other black women as if we all looked the same, like when Chief of Staff Donald Regan called me Zelda. I heard racial and misogynistic slurs and was unfairly stereotyped as someone who grew up in a disadvantaged neighborhood. I was labeled as "pushy" for simply speaking up in meetings and subjected to inappropriate jokes in the hallways. Whenever I expressed my discomfort, I was told to let it go and not be so sensitive.

Despite these challenges, I navigated the interconnected barriers of race and gender. The professional environment I encountered was designed to suppress diversity rather than foster it. Nevertheless, I persevered and drew strength from the accomplishments of those who paved the way before me. I owe my success to their hard work and dedication.

I needed help counting the number of diversity training programs I customized and conducted in the judiciary to address biases and prejudices. I made the sessions mandatory for managers and insisted they sign in to certify their attendance. My commitment to diversity training was based on the demographics and employee metrics that I collected and analyzed.

The Federal judiciary problems ranged from recruitment to retention and actions to behaviors. I tailored my training to the data yield without blaming the dominant group, but in the end, the programs were all a waste of time.

Irony

The judiciary remained a plantation mentality, elitism, and a bastion of overt racism. During my tenure from 1997 to 2014, the only way for a black person to work at the AO was if another black person recommended them for hire.

A black friend, Maurice White, who graduated from Harvard Law School, recommended me. No, he's not the Maurice White of Earth, Wind & Fire fame. Earth, Wind & Fire was a band with a new brand of pop music in the 1970s. The music was African and black styles of jazz, rhythm, and blues, and appealed to a broad cross-section of the listening public. Maurice White was the founder and leader of Earth, Wind & Fire. He embraced and helped bring about this evolution of pop, which bridged the gap between black and white America's musical tastes.

But I did know Maurice White of Earth, Wind & Fire. I met him at a promotional party in 1971 at the Denver Hilton Hotel, just before the band became a household name. I was friends with four members of the famous group in high school.

The saxophonist, Andrew Woolfolk, and I were in the East High School Band together. Andrew carried my bass, and I brought his sax. Philip Bailey, the lead singer, was a year behind me in school. Philip wanted to sing in the East High Senior Choir, but the director, Ms. Lynn said that he needed to sing better to be in the Choir.

Philip had a four-octave vocal range and a distinctive falsetto register. Yet, according to the white choir director, he didn't sing well enough. We all knew what this was about—the race quota thing—but Philip was a class act and took it in stride. Larry Dunn was three years behind me in school, so I needed to learn about him better. I recall he created Friends & Love, and Andrew, Philip, and Larry covered diverse genres to entertain Denver-area audiences.

Ralph Dickerson became the group's road manager. We had a shared connection at Shorter Church, where we had known each other since infancy. In a rather peculiar tradition,

WINNING THE BATTLE AGAINST MYSELF

our church held a Tom Thumb Wedding, a playful ceremony for young children. At the tender age of 3, I had the honor of playing the role of the bride, adorned in a wedding gown, while Ralph, at the age of 4, sported a dapper tuxedo as the groom. As the two-year-olds clumsily made their way down the aisle, flinging and munching on flower petals, the ring bearer had a mishap and burst into tears when the ring slipped from his grasp. To this day, Ralph humorously claims the title of my first husband when recounting this amusing anecdote to others.

The sequence of 'black hired at the AO only if another black recommended them' started when Rose Marie recommended her Harvard Law School colleague, Maurice White. Rose was the first black professional at the AO; I don't know how she got there. Maurice recommended Laura, a friend of his wife from Georgetown Law School. Maurice also recommended me. I, in turn, hired a long-time friend, Cecelia, a black Harvard Law School graduate acquaintance of Rose and Maurice. Once employed, we all did penance in an equal employment opportunity (EEO) shop.

When the director asked if I wanted an office on the 7th floor, the preferred floor because of its proximity to his office, I said, "No, that is unnecessary." I ended up with an office suite on the 5th floor—with the leftover carpet from the director's newly carpeted office.

In addition to having a peach-colored carpet in the director's office, the director also ensured that I was provided with a government book to choose new furniture. At that time, employees had not yet been given the opportunity to select furniture for their own office suites, as those were only reserved for top managers. One afternoon, while on the third floor, I came across a discarded couch in a dark turquoise color in one of the hallways. It only required some saddle soap to clean it up and restore its beauty. Following the appropriate procedures, I contacted housekeeping and was able to obtain the couch, which was now in excellent condition.

Irony

Additionally, I ordered two wingback chairs, four armchairs in complementary turquoise fabrics, and eight peach floral fabric chairs for my conference room. To complete the furnishings, I purchased tables and lamps, as well as two Islamic carpets. As a result, my office became a true showcase.

On my second day, Maurice took me to meet his boss, Rose. We sat outside her office for ten minutes, before her secretary ushered Maurice and me in. Rose was on the phone with her back turned to us. After more minutes of waiting, I told Maurice that we should leave. He gestured for me to whisper and remain seated. Rose heard me and turned around.

Her transparent, pathetic attempt to establish dominion over me, put me in my place, and make me her obsequious attendant, backfired. I never subjugated myself to anyone, no matter their race or gender. I was going to be a thorn in her unrealistic expectations, as she was a thorn with the name of the prettiest flower. Rose said I needed to come under her protection because the AO only valued loyalty.

The latter part of her statement was true. I soon learned that the AO was an insidious, soulless place. I told Rose that the former part of her statement was ludicrous: I'd been in the Reagan White House; I'd been an officer of the United States Senate where no one who was black or female had walked, so I certainly didn't need protection from her. I didn't even know her.

Maurice was such a good person. He deserved much more than Rose as a friend.

I was asked a question in the first meeting, which I attended with both of them. I don't remember the question, but I remember being kicked under the table by Rose. I held my temper, which was nearly impossible until after the meeting.

After the meeting, I found out why Rose kicked me.

When the room was cleared, I said, "If you ever touch me on any part of my body for any reason, I will kick your ass all over this building. Who the hell do you think you are—and, more importantly, who the hell do you think I am?"

WINNING THE BATTLE AGAINST MYSELF

She said, "You don't speak in meetings because you're educating them every time you open your mouth."

"Say what?!"

"Every time you speak; you are educating white people. We're smarter than white people. If you educate them, they will steal your ideas and claim they are their ideas. That will keep us down. Then they will rise to higher managerial posts."

Even if there was a shred of truth in her ramblings, Rose only cared about her career path—the career path that would never happen.

Rose never took into account who she was—a bully. She was unable to see how she was viewed. She was limited in her prospects because of who she was; she was never going to get out of the box she'd built around herself.

Precisely, what she feared came true, but she didn't understand the dynamics involved in bringing it about. She couldn't get past herself. Black people generally don't climb the professional ladder through lies, bullying, and intimidation. Even when we work hard to achieve upward mobility, more often than not, we are denied it.

To make the tension worse with Rose and other jealous blacks she had a grip on, the director called me to his office and told me he wanted me to be on senior staff and that I was to report directly to Rose's boss, not Rose.

I was shocked and confused. Senior staff was the plum meeting for high-level managers. When Rose found out, she tried the same approach with me that had failed before. She said that I should turn down the director's reporting structure and report directly to her because she was the only one who could protect me.

Really? Again? She was so ambitious and wanted to matter that she didn't understand why she would never get promoted.

During a private meeting, Pete, the deputy director, said, "I don't use those $50.00 words," the clear implication being that I used $50.00 words because I was more educated than he. I knew nothing of his education and couldn't care less, but

Irony

yes, with four degrees it was probable that I was more educated than him, but so what?

Pete said those things as a victimization tactic, a sacrificial ploy to sidestep his entrenched misogyny, classism, and racism.

I realized I was working under an authoritarian patriarchal regime.

During another meeting about Rose's mistreatment of me, Pete told me that Rose should have been fired "fifteen times or more," but "she was the primary breadwinner in her family and grew up in a way similar to how he grew up." He elaborated using similes like dirt poor, poor as a church mouse, lacking basics, etc. The inference being that I didn't grow up disadvantaged, but he and Rose had a commonality that surpassed her misanthropy. This management team must have spent time researching my background and forming biased opinions.

On April 2, 1999, the AO director, by memorandum, stripped me of my internal equal employment opportunity portfolio. I had fingered discriminatory and retaliatory managers within the AO, all white. The memorandum contained a phony compliment of my work, and the equal employment opportunity function went to the black person they could manipulate:

"With this move, the Employee Relations Office, under the highly capable leadership of Trudi M. Morrison will be able to focus all of its attention on providing policy support to the Judicial Resources Committee and support to the courts on EEO, fair employment practices, and employment dispute resolution systems."

I was aware that the black person they could manipulate stood up for me on more than one occasion. That's why I was surprised in August 2021, the black person they could manipulate turned on AO management and the courts. "I watched for over 20 years and what I saw, every step of the way, was the judiciary circling the wagons any time there was a complaint made by an employee... It was impossible for an employee to break through that," said the black person they could manipulate in a Washington Post story.

WINNING THE BATTLE AGAINST MYSELF

The black person they could manipulate joined a discrimination appeal filed in a court on August 20, 2021, saying, "[I] too faced discrimination—as a woman and as a black employee. She continued, "When somebody violates the rules, instead of holding them accountable, the judiciary makes sure nobody comes in and tells them what to do."

The black person they could manipulate compared judges to kings and queens with disparate approaches to running individual court chambers. She said, "The idea that the judiciary, a traditionally very conservative environment, could be progressive enough, self-aware enough to actually police themselves runs counter" to the culture in many courthouses.

This is from the black person they could manipulate, and they continually promoted over others, the one who did their bidding, the one who was their star. Did she face discrimination as a woman and as a black employee? It must have happened after my retirement in 2014 and before her retirement in 2017 because, to my knowledge, it certainly didn't occur during my 17-year tenure.

Chapter 24

Numbers Don't Lie

"In math, you're either right or wrong."
-Katherine Johnson

(When NASA used electronic computers for the first time-to calculate John Glenn's orbit around Earth-officials called on Katherine Johnson to verify the computer's numbers; Glenn had asked for her specifically and had refused to fly unless Johnson verified the calculations.)

In December 2020, I found myself at a crossroads of personal health and professional dedication. I underwent emergency heart surgery due to experiencing discomfort in my left arm, back, and neck. The symptoms were alarming-I was lightheaded and breaking out into cold sweats. On the morning of December 3, I went to my cardiologist, hoping for reassurance but preparing for the worst. He did several tests and promised to provide further information, leaving me in a state of anxious anticipation.

However, the day took an unexpected turn. As soon as I arrived at work, my cardiologist contacted me in a state of urgency. His words were brief but impactful: "Meet me immediately at Washington Hospital Center as soon as possible." That's all he said. I put down the phone and stared at the receiver, the weight of his words sinking in.

Cecelia, the black Harvard Law School graduate I hired, was in my office at the time. Without hesitation, she authoritatively said, "I'll drive you to the hospital." Her decisiveness was a stark contrast to my stunned immobility.

Cecelia took charge, demonstrating the kind of leadership I had always valued. She took my car keys, grabbed my hand to help me stand, and told Barbara, my secretary and friend, to follow us in her car.

At that moment, I was grateful for the support system I had built around me.

When we arrived at the Emergency Room, Cecelia's assertiveness proved invaluable. She checked me in and insisted that a cardiologist see me immediately. Her persuasiveness paid off—they placed me in a room within ten minutes. As I lay there, waiting for the next steps, I couldn't help but reflect on how my professional life had prepared me for moments of crisis like this.

Barbara, ever reliable, called my husband and parents. My mother, showing the same determination that had shaped my character, flew on the first available plane into Virginia Dulles, Reagan Washington National, or Baltimore Washington International. Her swift action meant she got to the hospital in time to see me before surgery. Her presence was a comfort, a reminder of the strength that runs in our family.

Surprisingly, I wasn't frightened or nervous about heart surgery. My faith, a cornerstone of my life, provided a sense of calm. I knew I was in God's hands. But even in this moment of personal crisis, my mind couldn't help but wander to the larger issues at stake in our nation.

In truth, I was more focused on the Supreme Court's decision as to whether Al Gore or George W. Bush would be president after the November 7, 2000 election. This preoccupation with national affairs, even in the face of personal health challenges, was characteristic of my lifelong commitment to justice and equality.

Numbers Don't Lie

Political intrigue or heart surgery was a challenging choice for me, but not for my doctors. They were focused solely on my health, while my mind grappled with the potential implications of the election outcome.

The situation was complex. Although Gore had conceded and rescinded his concession, the results were too close to call. Florida was the deciding state, and its recounting of votes had become a national spectacle.

I watched with a mixture of fascination and concern as people counted hanging chads, dimpled chads, and butterfly ballots. Some holes were partially punched out of ballots, adding to the confusion. Multiple legal challenges mucked up the works more. An electronic recount re-fed ballots into machines, but Gore demanded a hand recount.

The legal battle intensified. The Florida Supreme Court ordered a recount of under-votes (a ballot not counted because of unclear marking by the voter) in all Florida counties. Bush appealed to the U.S. Supreme Court. The High Court, seemingly reluctant to get involved, sent it back to the Florida Supreme Court.

When the Florida Supreme Court resumed its call for a recount, the case returned to the Supreme Court. Finally, on a 5-4 vote (nine people on the U.S. Supreme Court), the High Court declared that time had run out to find a remedy. Bush had more electoral votes than Gore, so he won. This decision would have far-reaching consequences for the nation, and I couldn't help but consider its implications even as I prepared for surgery.

Amidst this political turmoil and my health crisis, a personal drama unfolded. Maurice and Rose, with whom I hadn't spoken for two years, dared to show up at the hospital twenty minutes after my release and departure. Maurice called me later, inquiring about my health and informing me of the unexpected hospital visit. Their sudden appearance raised questions: Why did they come? What did they want? A cynical part of me wondered if they would have tripped over the heart monitor and said, "Oops"? Could their intentions have been even more sinister? I will never know, but their presence added an extra layer of tension to an already stressful situation.

Reflecting on my career, I recalled the challenges I faced in establishing a Heritage Celebration Series for the U.S. Courts. After pleading with the director on November 14, 1997, he sent a memorandum announcing "Heritage Celebrations," noting me as the contact person. What should have been a positive step towards inclusivity became a source of controversy. Black employees were told that my push to celebrate other cultures was motivated by my trying to eliminate the existing heritage celebration for blacks because I was a Republican. That was a lie, a painful misrepresentation of my intentions.

Another lie that circulated was that black employees would not get raises because of my influence. These falsehoods turned me into the enemy, and I noticed black employees began avoiding me. The atmosphere in the workplace became tense. Whenever I went to the pantry for lunch, they would be curt and many would even leave. It was a hurtful experience, one that highlighted the complexities of being a black woman in a position of authority.

It is important to note that every conflict I encountered was not related to race, but Rose's lies put race front and center. Rose was calculating and evil. I invited Rose to lunch to make peace. She declined, but I felt I had taken the high road.

Despite these challenges, I persevered in my efforts to bring diversity and inclusivity to the forefront. My American University teaching buddy, Julian Bond, agreed to keynote my first Black History Month. Julian was a prominent civil rights activist who became the first president of the Southern Poverty Law Center. Julian served as chairman of NAACP from 1998 to 2010 and was also active in politics in Georgia, serving in both chambers of the state's government for two decades. In 1998, Julian became chair of the NAACP board of directors, a job he referred to as "the most powerful job a Black man can have in America."

Numbers Don't Lie

For the first AO Women's History Month celebration in March, Justice Ruth Bader Ginsburg honored us by accepting my invitation. Her presence was a validation of the importance of our efforts. Justice Ginsburg was excited to be the first Women's History Month speaker for the Federal judiciary. She said she was proud of me and knew the celebration series must have been challenging to create, especially as a woman and a black woman. Her words were a balm to the wounds inflicted by office politics and misunderstandings.

However, not everyone shared Justice Ginsburg's enthusiasm. I was summoned to the director's office, where he threatened to discontinue the Heritage Series. To my surprise, the director was livid about my decision to bring in a civil rights icon and a Supreme Court Associate Justice who had played a key role in hiring the first woman Assistant Director at the AO.

Until this point, I had been completely unaware of the director's animosity towards my choices. He seemed to resent the fact that I had a better understanding of the key players and stronger political connections than he did. It appeared that he was simply threatened by my competence and knowledge. It was absurd that I was being accused of encroaching on his territory. It was clear that I had become a perceived threat.

This experience reinforced a truth I had long known: they had made the mistake of choosing the wrong person for a job they didn't want to accomplish…me. I was determined to continue my work, regardless of the obstacles placed in my path.

Approximately one year later, Pete, the white deputy at the Administrative Office of the U.S. Courts, called me on my private line. His call was indicative of the ongoing scrutiny and mistrust I faced.

"Have you had any recent contact with the top aide to the Chief Justice?" he asked, his tone implying suspicion.

"No," I replied truthfully. The Chief's top aide and I were friends and lunched occasionally, but I hadn't spoken to him recently.

WINNING THE BATTLE AGAINST MYSELF

Pete's next words were chilling: "Well, I called his top aide to inquire about your communication with the Court, and I'm waiting for a return call. It's 4:47 pm. and your future rests on the outcome of this call."

He hung up, leaving me to contemplate the implications of his threat.

Hearing nothing further, I left the office at 6:30 pm, uncertain of what the future held. A few months later, a memorandum from the director banned AO staff from direct contact with the Supreme Court. This ban was clearly aimed at limiting my influence and connections, a move that both frustrated and motivated me to find new ways to effect change.

One of the proudest achievements of my career was the hard-fought victory to write and apply reasonable accommodations for people with disabilities. The goal was to eliminate or minimize obstacles faced by employees with disabilities, enabling them to enjoy the same employment benefits and privileges as their non-disabled counterparts. This initiative was personal for me, as I often found myself in a wheelchair, on crutches, or using a cane to get around because of arthritis and a car accident.

During budget meetings, Pete, the AO deputy, interrogated me for five or six years. Each time I put forth budgetary analyses and common-sense arguments for assisting Federal court employees, including providing judges with personal readers, Pete would go into his incantation:

"Would personal readers help elderly judges get dressed, eat, walk up the stairs at home and in the courthouse? Would you give a personal assistant to a 93-year-old judge? Would we have to set aside parking spaces for handicapped employees? Would we have to spend money enlarging bathroom doors and stalls? Would we have to provide accommodations for an event an employee must attend that occurs off of our premises? Would we have to provide accommodations for probationary employees, etc.?"

Numbers Don't Lie

Pete's questions revealed a fundamental lack of understanding and empathy. He failed to grasp that disability was more the rule than the exception. His resistance was frustrating, but it only strengthened my resolve to push for necessary changes.

My personal experience with disability came to the forefront in October 2002 when I was rear-ended on the George Washington Parkway in McLean, Virginia. The car accident caused injuries that required me to work from home for several months. When I returned to my job, my boss repeatedly asked if I could travel to train court personnel. I consistently assured her I could continue traveling to conduct my training on employment dispute resolution and employment law. Her persistence in questioning my abilities bordered on discrimination. She went as far as asking if I considered disability retirement. In doing so, she set the AO up for a constructive discharge claim based on an offer of voluntary retirement that was, in fact, involuntary retirement.

The day before my departure, I received a call from Pete, the deputy director. He asked me to come to his office. I immediately became skeptical, as both Pete and the director had a history of having ulterior motives that were not in my best interest. Pete began the conversation with syrupy sweet platitudes:

"How are you feeling? You were missed. Your office only ran smoothly with you. The acting chief was a disappointment. Seeing you made my day. You're indispensable to us." His toxic positivity nauseated me.

"You know you may be rushing your recovery by traveling to the courts so soon," Pete said, his concern laced with ulterior motives.

"Thanks for your concern. I'll be alright," I responded, maintaining my composure.

"I don't want you to think we're putting pressure on you to get back out there."

"That thought never entered my mind, Pete."

"Our main concern is your health."

WINNING THE BATTLE AGAINST MYSELF

"Thanks. I'm fine."

Pete kept pressing, but I saw through his facade. Finally, I'd had enough.

"Pete, stop it. I've made it clear that I can travel to train court personnel. I know what you're up to. If I can't do the essential functions of my job-like travel, the AO is unable to provide reasonable accommodation for me, so dismissal is the only option. I created my job. There are no alternative accommodations, such as creating another job, working from home, reassignment, or a modified, or part-time work schedule. Even if you made up an alternative, you'd counter your own suggestion by claiming the alternative posed an undue burden on the AO, so dismissal is the only option. Your plan won't work. Remember, I wrote the reasonable accommodation guidelines and the reasonable accommodation roadmap."

Pete said nothing. I have never heard another word from Pete or my boss about a disability retirement. My knowledge of the system and the influence I earned by implementing Federal employment rights had protected me from their manipulations.

Through these experiences, I learned firsthand the discrimination and inequity one can encounter with a disability.

My staff and friends treated me differently when I was in my wheelchair. Some people would lean on my wheelchair, unaware that the wheelchair was an extension of my body or personal space. Others would say, "But you're so pretty," implying that being pretty doesn't 'go' with having a disability. These experiences only strengthened my resolve to fight for better understanding and accommodations for people with disabilities.

Pete seemed to forget that I had come from the Senate, where I had forged close relationships with several senators who were disabled. Senator Bob Dole's story of overcoming severe injuries from World War II, Senator Ted Kennedy's experiences with his sister Rosemary and son Teddy, Senator Orrin Hatch's brother-in-law's struggle with polio, Senator Dan Inouye's loss of his right arm in World War II, and Senator Tom Harkin's deaf brother-all these personal connections informed my understanding of disability issues and fueled my determination to make a difference.

While Pete set roadblocks to creating accommodations for the Third Branch of government, I worked tirelessly to write guidelines and a roadmap for reasonable accommodations for people with disabilities. To ensure their legal accuracy and sufficiency, I sought the expertise of Bob Loesche, the AO Deputy General Counsel, known for his brilliance as a lawyer. Eventually, after the director and Pete yielded, I wasted no time in publishing the guidelines and a roadmap providing a clear path and procedures that employees used to request and receive accommodations. Their surprise stemmed from the fact that I had already prepared these documents in advance, anticipating the eventual need for them.

Another contentious issue arose around drafting the Judiciary Fair Employment Practices Annual Report. The Report summarized judiciary data on gender, ethnicity, age, disability, court type, and employee claims across workforce occupational categories. My constant arguments for including the Supreme Court justices and their law clerk data continued to fall on deaf ears. The director's excuse was always the fear of the media finding out about the sparse/non-existent minority law clerks on the High Court. This resistance to transparency was frustrating, but I persisted in pushing for more comprehensive reporting.

I needed complete data from all Federal courts before drafting the Report. Then it went to Public Affairs for printing and publication. One day, I found myself in another confrontation in Pete's office. The head of Public Affairs, Dan, was sitting there when I arrived.

"Why isn't the Report completed yet?" Pete asked, his tone accusatory.

Dan chimed in, "Yeah, why isn't it?"

"Shut up, Dan," I said, gritting my teeth and holding my temper. "I won't finish the Report until I get all the data. I've spoken to the late courts and they're doing their best, Pete."

WINNING THE BATTLE AGAINST MYSELF

"If they've missed the deadline, don't include them in the Report," Pete suggested dismissively.

"I agree," Dan added, unhelpfully.

"Shut up, Dan," I repeated, my patience wearing thin. "No. I'm not going to exclude any courts unless waiting for them jeopardizes the layout and printing deadlines."

"Maybe you're being lackadaisical?" Pete insinuated.

"Were you speaking to me, Pete? Lackadaisical?" I asked, my anger rising.

Dan laughed, a sound from the darkest pits of Hell. "She must not know what lackadaisical means," he said, further stoking my ire.

My head turned to Dan like the girl in the 1973 Exorcist movie. "You half-witted son of a bitch! Shut your mouth, or I'll shut it for you!" I growled.

Dan was stunned. Pete looked amused.

"You'd better leave, Dan," Pete said, finally recognizing the tension in the room.

I turned to Pete, my frustration boiling over. "And you can kiss my ass!" I walked out of his office, leaving him to contemplate the consequences of their disrespect.

Weeks later, the Report was published, complete and accurate. Pete didn't hassle me about the Report again. My determination and refusal to compromise on quality had won out.

A couple of years later, my boss retired. I applied for her job; that would have made me Rose's boss. Rose also applied for the opening. Two people of the three on the interview panel told me I had been selected and that my name had been forwarded to Pete. I felt cautiously optimistic about this opportunity for advancement.

"Trudi, Pete wants to see you," his secretary said one day. I knew I had gotten the job, or so I thought. I confidently entered the suite occupied by the director and Pete, although my anticipated racism and sexism antenna was up.

"Go on in, Trudi," his secretary motioned.

Numbers Don't Lie

Pete didn't look up from his desk. "Do you know the biggest threat to a black professional?" he asked, his tone cryptic.

I was immediately on guard. "Is this another racist or sexist troupe, Pete? What do you want?" I wearily asked, bracing myself for whatever game he was playing.

"Another black professional," he stated, finally looking up at me.

I glared at him and headed for the door, disgusted by his attempt to pit minorities against each other.

"Your new boss is Alton, that's the same as my middle name," Pete said excitedly as if this revelation would somehow soften the blow.

The realization hit me hard. Once again, I had been passed over, despite being the most qualified candidate.

"You've done it again, Pete. Why bother with the farce of a selection committee, when you disregard its decision? I hope you told your namesake new guy that I will report to him directly because I won't report through Rose."

"That will be his choice. I can't tell him about his direct reports," Pete replied, feigning innocence.

"Since when Pete? You always rig the system in your favor without hesitation, so tell him I will not report through Rose. You don't want any trouble from me."

My words were a warning, thinly veiled. I knew the real reason behind this decision: Rose would have gotten the job if I hadn't applied. The interview panel selected me, but the AO couldn't afford an intra-racial, intra-gender battle, so they hired a white man, whom the panel couldn't even remember interviewing.

Time passed, and changes continued to occur in the office. The director announced his retirement. I waited to meet with the new director, curious about what this change might mean for my position and the initiatives I had worked so hard to implement.

Pete approached me as I sat on the sofa, waiting for my turn to meet the new director.

WINNING THE BATTLE AGAINST MYSELF

"Are you gonna tell him what a motherfucker I am?" he asked, his language surprisingly coarse.

I had never heard Pete cuss before. I was intrigued by this sudden shift in his demeanor.

"Gosh, golly gee, Pete. Why on earth would I say something like that? If you think I would say that about you, what have you told the new director about me?" I replied, my tone dripping with sarcasm.

Before Pete could respond, the secretary called out, "Trudi, Jim's ready. Come on in."

I smiled at Pete, leaving him to wonder about what I might say, and went into the new director's office, prepared to advocate for my work and my position.

Adding to the paradise I endured at the AO, a new crisis emerged: my secretary's husband threatened to kill me. The employee in question had been troublesome and had been moved from office to office. That's how I usually got my staff. Because the director and Pete didn't care about my office or me, they "gave" me employees no one else wanted. Please don't misunderstand. I didn't want them either, but I needed bodies to keep my office running.

Most hand-me-downs were incompetent, petty, gossiping, jealous troublemakers. This disaster of a secretary came to my office courtesy of the black person they could manipulate.

The AO was so afraid of complaints of discrimination and the media finding out that instead of firing people, it moved bad seeds around to pollinate other offices. I usually was the pollinated, forced to deal with problematic employees that no one else wanted to handle.

One day, during a staff meeting, I found myself having to raise my voice to keep order.

"Sheila, stop snoring! This is a staff meeting, wake up!" I yelled, frustrated by the lack of professionalism.

Another employee, CeCe, whom I didn't suspect of betrayal, went around the building bad-mouthing me so much that Pete called and told me he wanted her out of the building by the end of the day.

The irony wasn't lost on me—Pete and the director wanted me out, too, so this employee must have been saying truly horrible things about me to warrant such a reaction.

The challenges didn't stop there. One of my male employees was caught duplicating pornography on the copy machine, a clear violation of workplace policies. Another male employee used his government credit card for personal expenses—movies, dinners, flowers, perfume, and lingerie.

These incidents highlighted the ongoing issues I faced in managing a team that often seemed more interested in causing problems than in doing their jobs.

One particularly frustrating incident involved one of my professional employees, who was making a six-figure salary. She handed me a telephone message she had taken while I was in a meeting. The message read, "Trudi Morrison call Trudi Morrison." The absurdity of this situation would have been comical if it wasn't so indicative of the incompetence I was dealing with daily.

But the most alarming incident was yet to come. The secretary whose husband threatened to kill me shouldn't have been on my staff in the first place, but I needed a secretary and was often given problem employees that other departments didn't want.

This particular woman had an active imagination that viewed humans as animals, trees, stones, and plants. The Greek Orthodox Church was her life, and she repeatedly told me that her church was the only one that held the correct opinion on true Christianity.

One day, I asked her about a letter I had requested her to type two days prior. Her response was unexpected and alarming.

"I don't feel well," she said, evading the question.

"Do you need to go home?" I asked, concerned but also frustrated by her lack of productivity.

Suddenly, she started screaming at the top of her lungs.

WINNING THE BATTLE AGAINST MYSELF

"You spit on me! I'll show you!"

I was stunned. What just happened? She continued screaming, packing her belongings, and ran out of the office.

Bewildered and concerned, I immediately reported the incident to a specialist in the personnel office, seeking guidance on how to handle this bizarre situation.

"She's done this before. She's nuts. I'll send someone up to take the information," the specialist informed me, confirming my suspicions about the employee's unstable behavior.

But the situation escalated quickly. Within 10 minutes of her departure, I got a call on my private line from her husband. His words sent a chill down my spine: "I'm gonna kill you."

Shocked, I asked him to repeat himself, hoping I had misheard.

The phone went dead–a terrible choice of words given the circumstances. Shaken, I immediately called AO Personnel, Capitol Hill Police, and Metropolitan Police. The threat was real, and I needed to take it seriously.

The response was swift. The Capitol Hill Police were the first to arrive, obtaining the suspect's picture from his driver's license and sharing it within the Hill.

As the Capitol Hill Police Chief knew that I had previously been his boss, he gave priority to my case. The Metropolitan Police arrived next, with two officers visiting my office to gather further details about the incident.

I provided them with information about the employee's start date, assigned tasks, working hours, and leave history. I directed them to AO Personnel for any additional information they might need. They also possessed a photograph of the employee's husband, which would aid in their investigation.

AO Personnel advised me to work at home until the matter was resolved.

Living in Maryland, I asked if anyone had contacted Maryland law enforcement. They said no, but assured me they would take care of it. I left the office, my mind racing with the implications of this threat.

Numbers Don't Lie

When I got home, two police cars were in front of the house. Somehow, seeing those police cars made the situation real.

I felt a mix of relief and anxiety. I invited the officers in for coffee, an offer they accepted.

In my stressed state, I realized I didn't know how to make coffee. Why did I offer something that I didn't have and didn't know how to make? I must have panicked.

I stumbled through a dumb explanation, eventually serving water with or without ice. The officers were understanding and explained that they would pick up my secretary's husband and question him.

The husband tried to evade the police, but when they apprehended him, he repeated his threat to kill me.

I don't know what happened after that, but I worked from home for two months, constantly looking over my shoulder and wondering if the threat had truly passed.

When I returned to work, there were no incidents for several months. I began to relax, thinking the worst was behind me. However, one morning, I noticed my letter opener was severely bent and in a different place on my desk. Surveying my office, I saw my sofa had been ripped several times. The tears were long and jagged—the kind of shape that a letter opener would make. Alarmed, I called security.

They arrived quickly, taking photographs and lifting fingerprints. The next day, a hidden camera was installed directly outside my office, the door locks were changed, and a camera was placed in my office. I was cautioned to tell no one about the hidden camera. After months of surveillance, the camera revealed nothing, and no more incidents occurred.

However, the experience left me shaken and more aware than ever of the potential dangers that came with my position.

These personal threats and workplace challenges were set against the backdrop of larger systemic issues within the judiciary. Once in the sacred halls of justice, I found that judges constantly challenged me to show how smart I was—not just the pretty brown girl. There was always an undercurrent of doubt, a questioning of my qualifications. After all, was one of my four degrees from prestigious universities given to me through affirmative action? How about two of the degrees? Three?

That sideways glance, that whisper, that wink: I wouldn't get that sideways glance if I were working at the counter in Saks Fifth Avenue. Why would I have to explain or justify myself? The interrogations and suppositions took precisely 20 minutes before the judges would listen to what I had to say. I know the exact time because I timed them, a small act of defiance and self-preservation in the face of constant scrutiny.

The lack of equality of treatment toward black judges by white judges was real. I know because I was privy to behind-the-scenes conversations with many white judges.

During my tenure, I heard at least a dozen white Federal judges say negative things about black Federal judges: "We have to put some black judges on [this] committee or all hell will break loose;" "He must have gone to Howard Law School;" "Why do I have to send the AO information on how many minority judges we have?" "She always has a light caseload compared to the rest of us;" "Black judges are prone to rely on their values rather than objectivity when deciding cases."

These white judges could not understand that a diverse bench allowed them to draw on divergent life experiences and reflect on the communities they serve.

And consider the audacity, hubris, and disrespect these Federal judges had toward me to say these racist and sexist things in front of me. Some racist and sexist judges didn't know they were racist and sexist judges. That's why they were comfortable spewing racism and sexism around me. I was with them at breakfast, lunch, cocktails, and dinner and in between those times. They got comfortable with me, forgetting I was one of the people they were smearing.

I had to put these judges in check without hesitation each time I experienced the bite of their cruel words. Of course it didn't lessen their hate. They would simply avoid me for a couple of days. It made me wonder what they said when I wasn't present.

Plus, I suffered personal slights from a few judges. One judge told me that when he told his law clerks to jump, they responded, "How high?"

I said, "I'm not one of your law clerks."

This judge was Hispanic, and his attempt to intimidate me only strengthened my resolve to stand my ground.

Another judge inadvertently sent me an email intended for that same Hispanic judge, denigrating me personally and professionally. This judge was a white female.

That same white female judge asked me who I supported during the 2008 Democratic presidential primary with the existence of both a black and female front-runner. I asked her why she was asking me a political question. She said, "Because you are black and female. And, by the way, Obama is only half black."

Her words revealed the deep-seated biases that persisted even among those who should have known better.

I rejected buffoonery and subservience, which often put me at odds with my superiors. My boss joined the chorus of those who seemed to think the judges walked on water and were more than happy to find a reason to fire me. That was the overarching view of AO management. Those clowns. It took unwavering perseverance to deal with petty people each day when my mission was to help those who needed me to help them get equality of treatment.

It took a real human being who happened to be a white male judge from Maine, my mentor, and the most honorable man I knew, Judge George Singal, Judicial Resources Committee Chair, to tell the trio (the Hispanic male judge, the white female judge, and my boss) that I should have an opportunity to defend myself.

Of course, I needed no defense. I had created my place at the table and refused to get up, no matter how uncomfortable it made others.

WINNING THE BATTLE AGAINST MYSELF

The judiciary was terrified that the press would learn its secrets. It needed free rein to discriminate against employees in private.

Dan, AO public affairs chief, was the perfect foil for the judiciary. He was a puppet, dancing to whatever music the director and Pete played.

Congress's lack of interest in questioning the judiciary about its lack of diversity in the workforce and on the bench was equally disturbing and baffling.

Why didn't Congress insist on demographic data from the Supreme Court? In my seventeen years, of the 535 members of Congress, only one member, Representative Sheila Jackson Lee (D-TX), requested annual demographic data.

Another example of overt racial bias was the formation of an online law clerk application system. In 2004, I happened by an open door, overhearing plans to meet in the District Court to discuss "pilot" schools for the proposed online system. Pilot schools were the colleges and universities selected to try out the application system before taking it nationwide. The confab was to be held on August 4. I told my boss what I heard, knowing that this could be an opportunity to push for more diversity in the selection process.

Judge Robertson, chair of the Committee on Information Technology, called my boss to ask if she would attend his meeting the next day.

She informed him that "Trudi Morrison would be representing [her] due to scheduling conflicts."

When he expressed concern that [she] was sending an 'EEO rep,' [she] told him that [she] was sending [me] as [her] representative and that [I] was an attorney and had experience in teaching in a law school."

Judge Robertson "specifically requested that [I] not discuss judiciary matters at the meeting, citing it as inappropriate to air dirty laundry in public."

My boss "assured him that this would not be done."

The judge continued, "I am 'an old civil rights lawyer,' and I want the judiciary to be more inclusive in its hiring and to expand our diversity, but tomorrow's meeting isn't the time or place for this discussion."

My boss then asked him, "When such a discussion should take place?"

He responded, "The schools participating tomorrow are not necessarily the ones who will be part of the pilot program."

These exchanges raised several questions in my mind: Why would he think I would bring up judiciary matters regarding "dirty laundry?" What "dirty laundry" did the judiciary have? Why was the judge compelled to bring up his status as "an old civil rights lawyer" or his desire for inclusiveness and diversity? And why would my boss make assurances about me that she couldn't guarantee?

I knew Judge Robertson had advocated for increased diversity in the legal profession, so I was baffled by his conversation with my boss. I was aware of Judge Robertson's work with civil rights activist and business executive Vernon Jordan when Robertson co-led the Conference on Opportunities for Minorities in the Legal Profession. Perhaps the judge was aware that the judiciary had an abysmal record of efforts to diversify the bench and the workforce and felt the need to keep its disgrace under wraps.

I attended the meeting, determined to make my presence felt and to advocate for diversity, even if indirectly. I looked around the room for other people of color with whom to commune if not bond; none were there. I adjusted my comfort level accordingly, knowing that I would be the lone voice for diversity in this gathering.

The proposed pilot schools were Ivy League institutions - the elite. They were Brown University, Columbia University, Cornell University, Dartmouth College, Harvard University,

WINNING THE BATTLE AGAINST MYSELF

the University of Pennsylvania, Princeton University, and Yale University. It was a prototypical metaphor for white success: Go to Harvard. As the discussion continued, I raised "the diversity" question, knowing it needed to be addressed.

"Why are there no Historically Black Colleges and Universities with law schools in the pilot, especially with Howard University Law School 10 min (2.4 mi) via North Capitol St. N.W. from the AO? Their school of law advances and supports a diverse and inclusive environment that encourages academic excellence and community ..." I began, only to be interrupted by a white woman.

"We all know about Howard," she said dismissively.

I was not about to let this interruption silence me. "Oh, no you didn't–I wasn't finished and you are out-of-line interrupting me. So, you're telling me that what I'm saying has no value or interest to you."

"Oh, no, Dr. Morrison. I wasn't doing that. I'm sorry you interpreted it that way," she backpedaled, realizing her mistake.

"Yes, you did interrupt me and now you're playing the victimhood card. You inserted yourself into my talk because you think your interests are more important than anything I have to say. Your rudeness will not render me invisible or silent. All you've done is reveal your sense of entitlement and superiority."

A white man who arrived late chimed in and said, "I agree with Trudi. She's absolutely correct. Make sure there's diversity in the pilot program. That's essential. Howard's in."

I was grateful for the man's support. He tapped me on the shoulder and smiled as he left the room. I found out later that the man was Merrick Garland, Chief Judge of the U.S. Court of Appeals for the D.C. Circuit. Judge Garland later became the 86th Attorney General of the United States.

The program for which Judge Garland deserves credit was called the Online System for Clerkship Application and Review (OSCAR), which streamlined Federal law clerk and appellate staff attorney recruitment for judges, court unit administrators, recommenders, applicants, and law school administrators.

Numbers Don't Lie

I created a draft for the initial online program, named court participants for the working group, ensured law schools with large minority populations were included in the pilot, convened meetings, and ran the first web-based application system. The idea was to add diversity to judges' applicant pools and enable judges to manage many applications through search and sort features electronically.

While analyzing data, I discovered that a pipeline for law clerks existed, which allowed judges to ignore OSCAR. Clerkships were the gateway to becoming a judge, and this informal pipeline threatened to undermine the diversity efforts we were trying to implement.

"If signing up for OSCAR is discretionary, what will prevent judges from selecting law clerks from "feeder" schools, as they've done in the past?" I asked during the working group meeting, voicing my concerns.

"Nothing will prevent that," group members said, confirming my fears.

"What about judges seeking law clerks in schools under-represented in the past?" I pressed, trying to find a way to ensure diversity.

"Judges will continue to select law clerks from the schools they attended. You will never change that," group members said, their resignation palpable.

"So, you all are basically saying that if minority graduates want a clerkship, they must rely on a correlation between the ethnic make-up of the judge and their own ethnic composition. In other words, minority judges are more likely to select minority career and term law clerks, and minority attorneys are more likely to apply for law clerk positions with minority judges, or a combination of both?"

"Exactly," working group members agreed the stark reality of the situation laid bare.

When OSCAR became highly successful, AO management took responsibility out of my office.

WINNING THE BATTLE AGAINST MYSELF

In an OSCAR meeting, one of the white managers, Mel Bryson, who was part of the AO managerial cabal and married to the director's secretary, Cherry, said, "[Trudi] lacks the requisite skill set to run an automated system."

"Mel, you're an ass," I retorted, refusing to let his baseless criticism go unchallenged.

When I returned to my office, the woman who replaced the retired deputy, Pete, called me. She had been present at the meeting where the exchange occurred and had said nothing. Now, on the phone only because my boss had asked her to call me, she said, "I'm sorry if Mel's statement offended you." I pointed out two things: first, I was clearly offended, as evident by my response to Mel; second, her words didn't constitute an apology, as she had never expressed that Mel's words had offended her.

The next morning, Mel was waiting for me when I arrived at work. He had a rehearsed apology, which he must have worked on overnight, and he used the word "inartfully" three times.

The irony of Mel's statement and the white woman deputy's non-apology wasn't lost on me. My "skill set" for managing a web-based system spanned 17 years at the AO, during which I had compiled and analyzed data to identify demographic similarities, disparities, and trends encompassing all facets of personnel management. I had also drafted 17 Judiciary Fair Employment Practices Annual Reports. It was clear that Mel's comment and the deputy's non-apology were motivated by something other than an honest assessment of my abilities.

These experiences led me to reflect deeply on how racism and sexism impact women of color in professional settings. The answer was clear: adversely, by planting pervasive doubts about competence, intelligence, and skill unrelated to actual performance. My experiences have shown that efforts to achieve more gender diversity often meant that black women got the short end of the stick unless race or ethnicity was explicitly stated.

White women have disproportionately benefited from affirmative action policies based solely on gender. I don't believe white women have it easy in our society, which is predominantly dominated by white males. However, it is important to acknowledge that black women are too easily ignored with the banality that tries to advance the representation of women without analyzing which women are most likely to benefit.

Judge George Singal, Chief Judge of the United States District Court for Maine, was in company with Judge Garland's integrity and fairness. Judge George Z. Singal was born in a World War II refugee camp after his mother and sister escaped Poland. Judge Singal co-founded and chaired the Diversity Ad Hoc Subcommittee of the Judicial Conference of the United States, along with my friend, Judge Wiley Daniel. On more than one occasion, I witnessed Judge Singal admonish other judges who disrespected staffers. His commitment to fairness and respect was a beacon of hope in an often-challenging environment.

In 2010, Judges Daniel, Singal, and I created a Diversity Recruitment and Outreach Program for Federal judicial interns and law clerks. We collaborated with the Just the Beginning Foundation–A Pipeline Organization of black judges to start a Summer Judicial Internship Diversity Project. The project placed highly qualified, diverse law students in judicial internships to increase the pipeline of various candidates for Federal clerkship positions and, potentially, Federal judgeships. This initiative was a step towards addressing the systemic lack of diversity in the judiciary.

The internal (AO) struggle to recognize the criticality of racial diversity in the Federal judiciary workforce was brutal. There wouldn't have been a Diversity Ad Hoc Subcommittee of the Committee on Judicial Resources if I hadn't proposed it to Judges Daniel and Singal. Despite my forming and staffing the subcommittee, my boss wanted to keep me from attending subcommittee meetings.

Perhaps, my boss lost her mind and lapsed into believing that she controlled my thinking, as Dr. Carter G. Woodson

WINNING THE BATTLE AGAINST MYSELF

wrote in Mis-Education of the Negro, a book originally published in 1933:

"When you control a man's thinking, you do not have to worry about his actions. You do not have to tell him not to stand here or go yonder. He will find his 'proper place' and will stay in it. You do not need to send him to the back door. He will go without being told. In fact, if there is no back door, he will cut one for his special benefit. His education makes it necessary."

My boss's attempt at control peaked on November 14, 2008. "Maybe we could set [the phone call] for 11 am and patch you in by phone," she wrote. Note the word 'wrote.' Not even the decency to tell me in person.

"By phone? When and why was it decided that I'm not going to the JRC in December?

...I'm at a loss to understand why I wasn't even consulted about ad-hoc subcommittee meetings on Monday before the full body meets. What's going on?" I wrote—no response from my boss.

Coincidentally, I received an anonymous fax showing the data my boss and a sycophant presented to the full Committee on Judicial Resources. My numbers had been changed to put the judiciary workforce and the judiciary judge demographics in a better light regarding racial and ethnic diversity.

The racial diversity in the judiciary was so abysmal that those who controlled access to the truth would lie, forge, alter, deny, and forbid its internal and public airing.

My debased, honest work was printed on paper that bore the name of Kinko's, a fast-printing service.

I conveyed my disgust to my boss and her sycophant when they returned to the AO following the JRC meeting. My boss was reduced to tears. She wasn't upset that I had uncovered her treachery; she was upset because I confronted her while her comrade-in-dirt, her underling, was present.

I tried to get the truth out again. I proposed an article on diversity in the Federal judiciary's newsletter, The Third Branch. On November 20, 2008, my boss wrote, "I spoke with

Numbers Don't Lie

[Public Affairs—[Dan] about a diversity article. [Public Affairs] explained the difficulty with using The Third Branch. It goes to 11,000 recipients including Congress and the press so it is risky to use this vehicle to communicate about the need for more diversity. However, [Public Affairs] will develop a fact sheet of options which I will take to the meeting which [Public Affairs] can address when you call in for the subcommittee mtg.," she wrote.

"Did [Public Affairs] mention the need for information about the subcommittee efforts in order to develop the fact sheet of options?" I wrote, trying to ensure that the full scope of our diversity efforts would be represented.

On November 21, 2008, my boss wrote, "I don't believe so. To [Public Affairs], the issue is exposure outside of the judiciary and the subcommittee needs to understand that."

I was not satisfied with this response. "I understand the circulation issue, but of more importance is conveying that use of this vehicle (The Third Branch) is NOT risky as a means to communicate our commitment, successes, and efforts toward maintaining and enhancing the strides we've made through the subcommittee's involvement. 'Risky' and 'difficulty' are not words that [Public Affairs] or you or any of us should use regarding the subcommittee's interest in diversity. Not writing an article would mean that we think diversity = Bad, Negative, or Not Enough. Please don't bring this to them in a light that implies that diversity means something negative to any of us; therefore, we'd write about the need for more diversity or that we have no diversity or that we have less diverse nonpolitical judge appointments, etc., this is our cornerstone on which we will continue to build a workforce that reflects the communities we serve. The article is intended to inform judges that diversity is a priority and that we are doing very good things, i.e., diversity = Good, Positive, Continued Efforts." No response from my boss.

Ultimately, there was no article about diversity in The Third Branch. The compromise was doing a question-and-answer piece on Judge Singal, whereas one of the questions posed was, "How does the Committee plan to increase diversity in the federal Judiciary?"

I revised the draft attempt by [Public Affairs], and, according to my boss, the article went "to print without an interview being conducted." My revisions were dated January 23, 2009; I raised the idea of a diversity article on November 20, 2008; the article was 16 lines long—three months for 16 lines. The glacial pace of progress was frustrating, but I refused to give up.

In 2007, I wrote letters, fact sheets, and statistics for the committee chairs of bankruptcy judges, magistrates judges, and court unit executives. My idea was to promote diversity on the bench by having the Judicial Resources Committee partner with those groups through joint signatures whenever the selection process is initiated to fill a bankruptcy or magistrate judge vacancy.

I sent the diversity letters, fact sheets, and statistics to my boss on July 15, 2008, and again on November 21, 2008. Judges requested such letters be written at the JRC meeting on December 2, 2008. My boss didn't tell them I had already written the letters. One of the JRC judges called and informed me of the requested work. I faxed her copies of varied letters to distribute to the committee members. I told my boss of the request and my response. She looked at me with resentment and said nothing.

I proposed a recruitment video to show at job fairs and other events. In a December 9, 2008 email, Dan argued for "delaying the release of the recruitment video until the employment page on the uscourts.gov website is up and running."

My boss didn't believe it was appropriate to wait.

"The I.T. development may or may not be ready in 6 months," she wrote.

On the same day, I wrote to my boss, "Although [Dan] didn't include me in his email, he forwarded it to me. You... made a call in which you didn't ask for my input, nor did you copy me on your response to [Dan]–a quick email simply asking me yea or nay..." Why would people fail to include me in emails affecting a suggested project?

This "aggressive, angry, persistent, arrogant, self-important, uppity" black woman gave the Federal judiciary a lot: reasonable accommodations and personal assistants (i.e., readers for the blind and interpreters for the deaf) for employees and judges with disabilities; annual reports on the status of fair employment practices; the heritage celebration series; a process to implement employment dispute resolution procedures; a Diversity Subcommittee of the Judicial Conference of the United States; OSCAR, from its inception with Article III Ventures, Inc. criticizing the process used to award OSCAR to Simplicity Corporation, to the appointment of a Court Collaboration Group, to the selection of the OSCAR Working Group members, and to providing a seamless transition for OSCAR to the AO; outreach and recruitment efforts; judicial salaries; cancellation or postponement of Federally insured student loans; and the development of the Summer Law Clerk Extern Program.

Judge Damon J. Keith, the grandson of enslaved people and the longest-serving black judge in the nation, and a civil rights icon, upon notification of my retirement on February 21, 2014, wrote:

> *"Dear Trudi: ...Your contributions have made dreams come true for many. As a true champion of diversity in the courts, you helped develop the Just the Beginning Summer Law Clerk Extern Program, and to date, hundreds of diverse students can thank you for their placements in federal judicial chambers. By putting your commitment to diversity into practice, and by achieving meaningful results, you have set an illustrious example for lawyers and jurists to follow, as we continue to strive for greater diversity in this nation's federal courts.*
> *I know that you will be missed by your colleagues, as you have been an inspiration for many, and your work leaves behind a formidable legacy to which others will aspire*

for generations to come. You are to be commended for many jobs well done. Please accept my congratulations, my thanks, and my admiration.
With best wishes, D.K."

I've thought long and hard about something—anything that I could say that would be positive about the Federal judiciary. Other than a paycheck and a pension, some very generous and thoughtful people donated leave during my illnesses. For that, I sincerely thank them.

I only believed in staying at the party briefly, although the AO was as far from a party as possible. The motivation to retire came during a senior staff meeting. I looked around the room and realized I was older than most colleagues. When I started working there, I was one of the youngest managers on the senior staff—the time had come to retire, although the idea of retirement frightened me. I experienced the fear of severance. What should I do every day? After my high-profile jobs in each branch of our national government, would I find any more challenges? How would I find my relevance again? All my clothes were business suits; would I have to buy a wardrobe of jeans and sneakers? How should I handle curious people who are intrigued with my public life and want to chat about it? Would my future be diminished? Would anyone care about the experience I accumulated? Would I have a profound loss of identity? Would I require reassurance of my value as a human being?

I needed to ease into retirement. I negotiated a year's salary in 2013 while working out of my home in Colorado—an unprecedented, groundbreaking achievement. I officially retired on February 28, 2014.

Retirement

I spent two years at home in Denver with my Daddy after retirement. His final months coincided with the birth of my great-niece, Zoe, who was six months old when Daddy passed.

Ronnie, my early crush and now my husband, and I cared for Zoe during the day. We witnessed her "firsts"–rolling over, sitting up, crawling, talking, and walking. While Zoe was getting stronger, Daddy was getting weaker. He passed away on Mother's Day 2015. Losing him will always cause me unbearable emotional anguish.

And There Were Blessings
My niece, Simone, was born in 1982, bringing immeasurable joy and pride into my life. Simone was always the apple of my eye. She was the daughter I never had. Simone married Ryan in 2007; they had Gavin in 2009 and Zoe in 2014. Vicki blessed us with Simone, and Simone blessed us with Gavin and Zoe. I was there for Zoe's birth. Ronnie and I cared for Zoe in the daytime during her first year. God gave me a second chance. I had trouble letting her go when Ryan and Simone put her in daycare.

Dreams are made of Zoe's caramel skin, big dark eyes with bright white sclera, long black lashes, and thick, curly hair. Her beauty leaves me breathless. Watching her grow and learn gives my life meaning. My love for her is endless.

I often wonder what Zoe's life will be like. She has a history of strong black women in her family. Her pathway has been forged. I knocked down many doors for her. I took control of my narrative so I wouldn't be erased.

I will teach Zoe to control her narrative and defy those who say she is less than. Racism has not significantly improved in my life despite the efforts of many who preceded me and my work. I am still alive, so hope remains that racism and sexism may marginally abate during my lifetime.

Like me, Zoe will grow up black and female. Unfortunately, I don't think racism and sexism will disappear in her lifetime or the lives of her children or grandchildren. I believe those ills will be more or less overt and covert throughout her time. I will teach her not to trust those hidden times because they will be an illusion.

WINNING THE BATTLE AGAINST MYSELF

She will not overcome racism or sexism. But Zoe will learn to deal with them ... and thrive. Her spirit is strong. She will learn self-confidence and self-control.

I will also teach her not to hate. Hate will only destroy her. I will say racism is wrong and that she did not do something to deserve to be treated poorly.

As she grows and cements her sense of identity, I will urge her to choose a life of acceptance, compassion, service, and respect for fellow human beings. I will make it clear that I didn't condone bias or stereotypes. I will teach her to defend herself against physical and mental abuse and always tell her the truth.

Zoe is an intense learner and very competitive. She takes great pride in being a girl. I do not doubt that as a role model for her, she will value public service and be highly successful in work and all aspects of her life. May her little heart have courage.

Chapter 25

Conclusion

"If you know what you're talking about, or if you feel that you do, the reader will believe you."
-Nikki Giovanni

But for this book, you may not have known me. It is a fallacy that where one comes from determines who one is. My life was work, the school of hard knocks. I am a testament to "Black Girl Magic."

This magic isn't just about success; it's about resilience. Black Girl Magic doesn't allow you to give up, even when the world seems determined to push you down.

It took me 30 years to get to the White House, 35 years to get to the Senate, nearly 50 years to get to the Administrative Office of the United States Courts, and more than 70 years of education and experience to write this book. Each step was a battle, each achievement hard-won against a system that often seemed designed to exclude me.

Still, I needed more time. Writing this book made me realize a part of my life that I kept hidden. For most of my life, I was depressed, insecure, vulnerable, and disposable. As Tananarive Due writes in The Reformatory, page 78,

WINNING THE BATTLE AGAINST MYSELF

"Was this all life was? A series of experiences, and then someone feeding you as if none of it had ever happened? As if you'd never left any impression on the world? [I] felt an unlived version of [my] life sailing away, out of grasp."

These words resonated deeply with me, capturing the essence of my struggle to make a lasting impact in a world that often seemed indifferent to my existence.

No one needed me. I was amazed that I was able to function, let alone achieve and encourage others. This constant feeling of being superfluous was a weight I carried throughout my career, invisible to those who saw only my accomplishments.

Paradoxically, my greatest strength was being underestimated. Hiring authorities always picked the wrong person for the job they didn't want to do—me. They viewed me as the "check-off candidate."

- Black: check.
- Female: check.
- Educated: check.
- Presentable: check.
- Articulate: check.

Little did they know that in hiring me, they were getting so much more than a set of superficial qualities. They were getting a force for change, a voice for the voiceless, and a tireless advocate for justice and equality.

The glamor and thrill of imagery are nothing like reality if you're a competent, sincere person doing a professional, honest job. Newspapers and magazines printed pictures of me in beautiful gowns. They were the façades; that was the window dressing. Yes, my consequential role was complicated by my race and sex. But I refused to dampen aspects of my personality so I could fit into the culture of my workplace. My quest was to rid blacks and whites of the notion that significance can only be determined by white society or white privilege. This quest often felt Sisyphean, as I pushed against entrenched attitudes and systems day after day.

Conclusion

Dealing with the endless repetitiveness of oppression exhausted me. Each small victory was hard won, each setback a reminder of how far we still had to go. Yet, I persevered, drawing strength from the knowledge that my struggles were paving the way for those who would come after me.

My significance largely came from the early influences of music and art. Are the best music and the best art made from pain? I don't know. I never equated the pain of discrimination with the beauty of music and art. But perhaps there's a connection—both require a deep well of emotion, a willingness to confront difficult truths, and the courage to express oneself authentically.

I know my story is not of black America but of America. It's a story of the complexities and contradictions of our nation, of the progress we've made and the long road still ahead.

At its core, despite all those things, when I walked into a room, some people only saw a black person, and some others only saw a woman. I wasn't in other people's minds, so I didn't know how they'd react. I only knew that I made sure that favorable treatment was the only treatment I would accept. This determination to be treated with respect was both a shield and a sword, protecting me from discrimination while also challenging those around me to confront their own biases.

I'm not sure this book will help anyone. There's not much optimism in it. It shows that the road less traveled is fraught with rejection, "otherness," disrespect, humiliation, and sorrow. But in showing these harsh realities, perhaps it can serve as a beacon for those who find themselves on similar paths, a reminder that they are not alone in their struggles.

Truth is seldom positive. But I've shown you that. My advice: Go for it anyway! There's always hope. And where there's hope, there may be change. You'll be a blessing to many you will never meet. Your actions, your perseverance, your refusal to be silenced or sidelined—these things ripple outward, touching lives in ways you may never know.

WINNING THE BATTLE AGAINST MYSELF

One day my great-niece, Zoe, said to me, "Tutu, you used to be President, and now you take orders from a five-year-old."

Out of the mouths of babes. This innocent observation captures so much–the cyclical nature of life, the humbling experience of caring for a child, and perhaps most poignantly, the hope that the next generation will build upon the foundations we've laid, reaching heights we could only dream of.

As I conclude this memoir, I'm reminded that our stories don't end with our last achievement or our retirement. They continue in the lives we've touched, the changes we've fought for, and the legacy we leave behind. My journey, with all its trials and triumphs, is now part of a larger narrative–one of progress, resilience, and the ongoing struggle for equality. It's a narrative that will continue long after I'm gone, carried forward by the Gavins and Zoes of the world and all those who dare to dream of a more just and equitable future.

Figure 25. -Great-nephew and -niece Gavin and Zoe, 2018.

Acknowledgments

To Allan Kassirer,
For more than 50 years you have been one of my closest friends. You are my trusted confidant and wise counsel. There would not be a book without your support and referral to Joel Engel, a master at pulling a story out of me. Thank you, Allan.

To Joel Engel,
You were patient and professional through 18 interviews. You subtly forced my explicit memories of episodic events. You have a light touch while probing to promote and explore my critical thinking and thoughts and feelings. I am deeply indebted to you. Thank you, Joel.

To Carolyn Walker,
You were my first editor who offered invaluable critiques of my drafts. You wrote an easy read in "Every Least Sparrow" (Garn Press). Thank you, Carolyn.

To Sacha Francois Heppell,
You opened a new digital world for me throughout the arduous task of writing. You asked author Marie Still to review my manuscript. You are a true friend to my family and me. Thank you, Sacha.

To Marie Still,
You are a reader and writer of books. You offered excellent suggestions to improve my manuscript. I enjoyed your books, "We're All Lying," "My Darlings," and "Beverly Bonnefinche is Dead." Thank you, Marie.

To Kevin Anderson & Associates,
Mark Weinstein, Editorial Director, SVP
Stephen S. Power, Executive Editor
Lauren Downey, Project Manager, Editorial
Molly Riggs, Operations Coordinator

You are a super efficient clan that produced my desired effects. Your competency is a part of your ethos. Thank you, Mark, Stephen, Lauren, and Molly.

To Writing and Editing Mentors,
Anna Jones
Sienna Rogers
Leo Burton
Austin Blake
Lucas Shaw

You guys worked tirelessly to distill my manuscript into a polished text and design my book cover and create my on-line presence. I want to particularly thank Sienna and Lucas for your weekly updates to assuage my anxiety. Thank you, Anna, Sienna, Leo, Austin, and Lucas.

To Journey Institute Press,
Michael Jenet, Publisher and Dafna Michaelson Jenet,

What a fabulous team you make. I am humbled that you see my dream as worthy of your talents. Thank you, Michael and Dafna.

Family

To my parents, George and Marjorie Morrison, because they loved me. This book is for them, too. May you both rest in the arms of our Lord.

To my sister, Vicki, for listening to my daily and nightly incoherent ramblings and making sense of them, as well as assisting with memories of our family legacy. You believe in me even when I doubt myself. Thank you, VJ.

To my cousin, George, for your infatigable patience and indomitable spirit. Your confidence in me never wavers. For years you've encouraged me to write a book. I finally did it. Thank you, Georgie.

To my niece, Simone, for introducing me to my publisher, Michael Jenet, and offering unsolicited advice that was consistently insightful and helpful. Thank you, Precious.

To my great niece, Zoe, who is the greatest assistant/agent anyone could ask for. Your humor and wisdom belie your young years. You keep me grounded and on-task. You are the reason for this book. Thank you, Angel.

I bear full responsibility for any errors in fact or judgment in this book.

-TMM

ABOUT THE AUTHOR

Dr. Morrison is the only person to have served in top posts in all three branches of the national government. She served the Reagan administration as associate director of the White House Office of Public Liaison and director of the 50 States Project, which studied discrimination in state laws and regulations based on gender. In 1985, she made history by becoming the first woman and the first Black Officer to serve as Chief Operating Officer and Deputy Sergeant at Arms of the United States Senate. In 1997, she headed the Fair Employment Practices Office and served as Senior Legal and Policy Advisor at the Administrative Office of the United States Courts, a role in which she was responsible for developing, implementing, and monitoring the Fair Employment Practices Program in the Federal Judiciary. Now retired, Dr. Morrison has commendations from four U.S. presidents, two Senate majority leaders, two chief justices, and three United States Supreme Court associate justices.

She is a fifth-generation Coloradan, a fifth-generation African Methodist Episcopal Church member, and a former fifth-generation Republican. In Denver, there is a park named after her grandfather, George Morrison Sr., who was dubbed "Denver's Godfather of Jazz." He was a legendary musician who played with Paul Whiteman, William "Bojangles" Robinson, Nat "King" Cole, Count Basie, Jelly Roll Morton, and Duke Ellington. On October 17, 2023, her grandfather was inducted into the Colorado Music Hall Of Fame. Her father, George Morrison Jr., was a school principal and administrator in the Denver public schools; her mother was an executive to eight Denver mayors. Her cousin, George Morrison Bailey, was the rehearsal pianist for the Stuttgart Ballet for forty-one years.

Dr. Morrison has earned four degrees: a Bachelor of Science from Colorado State University, a Juris Doctor from the National Law Center at George Washington University, and a Master's Degree and Ph.D. from the University of Michigan. She treasures her status as CSU's first recipient of the William E. Morgan Alumni Achievement Award in 1984. This award is the highest honor given and reserved for alums who have excelled nationally or internationally. This award aims to recognize a Colorado State University graduate who has attained extraordinary distinction and success in their field of endeavor and whose achievements have brought credit to Colorado State University and benefit their fellow citizens.

She lives outside Denver in Aurora, Colorado.

JOURNEY INSTITUTE PRESS

Journey Institute Press is a non-profit publishing house created by authors to flip the publishing model for new authors. Created with intention and purpose to provide the highest quality publishing resources available to authors whose stories might otherwise not be told.

JI Press focusses on women, BIPOC, and LGBTQ+ authors without regard to the genre of their work.

As a Publishing House, our goal is to create a supportive, nurturing, and encouraging environment that puts the author above the publisher in the publishing model.

Storytellers Publishing is an Imprint of Journey Institute Press, a division of 50 in 52 Journey, Inc.

NOTE: The world of publishing has changed dramatically. This has also affected authors and their ability to let readers know about their books. Today, most people buy books based on word of mouth.

If you would like to help this author, please consider leaving an honest review of this book on retail sites and book community sites.

www.ingramcontent.com/pod-product-compliance
Lightning Source LLC
Chambersburg PA
CBHW022026050526
44107CB00118B/1301/J